GLUTEN-FREE ARTISAN BREAD

in Five Minutes a Day

GLUTEN-FREE ARTISAN BREAD

in Five Minutes a Day

The Baking Revolution Continues with 90 New, Delicious, and Easy Recipes Made with Gluten-Free Flours

JEFF HERTZBERG, M.D., and ZOË FRANÇOIS

Photographs by STEPHEN SCOTT GROSS

THOMAS DUNNE BOOKS

ST. MARTIN'S PRESS ❧ NEW YORK

This book does not provide medical advice; its content and suggestions do not substitute for consultation with a physician. Medical and nutritional science change rapidly, and information contained in this book might not be current when read. Neither the publisher nor the authors are liable for any loss, injury, or damage arising from information in this book, including loss or injury arising from typographical errors.

THOMAS DUNNE BOOKS.
An imprint of St. Martin's Press.

GLUTEN-FREE ARTISAN BREAD IN FIVE MINUTES A DAY. Copyright © 2014 by Jeff Hertzberg and Zoë François. All rights reserved. Printed in the United States of America. For information, address St. Martin's Press, 175 Fifth Avenue, New York, N.Y. 10010.

Photographs copyright © 2014 by Stephen Scott Gross

www.thomasdunnebooks.com
www.stmartins.com

Designed by Phil Mazzone

Library of Congress Cataloging-in-Publication Data

Hertzberg, Jeff.
    Gluten-free artisan bread in five minutes a day : the baking revolution continues with 90 new, delicious and easy recipes made with gluten-free flours / Jeff Hertzberg, MD, and Zoë François; Photographs by Stephen Scott Gross.
        pages cm
    ISBN 978-1-250-01831-1 (hardcover)
    ISBN 978-1-250-01830-4 (e-book)
    1. Gluten-free diet—Recipes. 2. Bread. 3. Cooking (Bread) I. François, Zoë. II. Gross, Stephen Scott, illustrator. III. Title.

    RM237.86.H47 2014
    641.5'638—dc23

                                                                        2014022132

St. Martin's Press books may be purchased for educational, business, or promotional use. For information on bulk purchases, please contact Macmillan Corporate and Premium Sales Department at 1-800-221-7945, extension 5442, or write specialmarkets@macmillan.com.

First Edition: October 2014

10 9 8 7 6 5 4 3 2 1

To our friends and readers, who inspired us to create tasty gluten-free breads

J.H. and Z.F.

CONTENTS

ACKNOWLEDGMENTS

Gluten-free baking isn't quite the same as wheat-flour baking. We lived through a steep learning curve with friends and colleagues who lent their support, advice, and test kitchens to us. We couldn't have done it without them:

Heartfelt thanks go to Sarah Kieffer (TheVanillaBeanBlog.com), whom you already know from her beautiful work on our website—Sarah's been helping us for a while now, and also acted as our photo stylist for the photographs in this book. Moral and material support came from Kathy Kosnoff and Lyonel Norris, Craig and Patricia Neal, Lorraine Neal, and Jennifer Sommerness. Jeff Lin of BustOutSolutions.com maintains our ever more complex reader website, BreadIn5.com, which was created in 2007 by Graham (Zoë's husband). Laura Silver (Jeff's wife) continues to read and tweak every word we write with the eye of a professional editor. Thanks to Fran Davis and Barb Davis for all of their support. Peggy Orenstein and Beth Fouhy have helped us understand the magical world of literary public relations since our first book release in 2007—we wouldn't be here without them.

Thanks go to Pete Wolverton, Amelie Littell, Leah Stewart, Mary Willems, Elizabeth Curione, Nick Small, Marie Estrada, Kerry McMahon,

Christy D'Agostini, Anne Brewer, Karlyn Hixson, and all the folks at Thomas Dunne Books who've made our series a reality. And to Judy Hunt, who created another fantastic index. Our literary agent, Jane Dystel, and her team at Dystel and Goderich were by our side as always, helping us to navigate the ever-changing publishing industry.

Gratitude to colleagues in our baking, culinary, and medical worlds past and present: Shauna James Ahern of GlutenFreeGirl.com; the good folks at Bluestar Cooking; Steven Brown of Tilia; Robert Dircks, Alan Stoffer, and their team at Gold Medal Flour, including the Doughminators—Bill Weekley and Tim Huff; Stephen Durfee of the Culinary Institute of America; Dr. Alessio Fasano of Harvard Medical School; Barbara Fenzl of Les Gourmettes Cooking School; Thomas Gumpel of Panera Bread; Bill Hanes and Kelly Olson of Red Star Yeast; Nicole Hunn of GlutenFreeOnAShoestring.com; Brenda Langton of Spoonriver restaurant and the Minneapolis Bread Festival; Stephanie Meyer of FreshTartSteph.com; Silvana Nardone; Karl Benson and the folks at Cooks of Crocus Hill; Suvir Saran and Charlie Burd of American Masala; Tara Steffen of Emile Henry cookware; Andrew Zimmern, Dusti Kugler, and Molly Mogren of Food Works; Dorie Greenspan; Tom Wiese and Pace Klein of Wiese Contract Studio; and Dr. Stefano Guandalini, medical director of the University of Chicago Celiac Disease Center, who helped us sort through some of the more confusing and controversial issues regarding wheat and health.

Special thanks to our photographer, Stephen Gross, who once again found beauty in round brown disks. Thanks also to Nanci Dixon, prop stylist Veronica Smith, and the folks at the General Mills photo studios for the use of their state-of-the-art facilities and prop warehouse. Most of all, we are thankful for the love and support of our families: Zoë's husband, Graham, and her two boys, Henri and Charlie, and Jeff's wife, Laura, and his girls, Rachel and Julia. They're our best taste testers and most honest critics.

THE SECRET

Gluten-Free Dough Stores Well in the Refrigerator

It is so easy to have freshly baked gluten-free bread when you want it, with only five minutes a day of active effort. First, mix a large batch of dough and let it sit for about two hours. Now you are ready to shape and bake the bread, or you can refrigerate the dough and use it over the next five to ten days. Each recipe makes enough dough for many loaves. When you want fresh-baked gluten-free bread, take a piece of the dough from the container and shape it into a loaf. Let it rest for about 60 minutes, depending on the recipe, and then bake. Your kitchen will be as fragrant as a French bakery, and your gluten-free loaves will be far superior to any you can purchase at the store.

1

INTRODUCTION

Making Gluten-Free Bread in Five Minutes a Day: Refrigerating Pre-Mixed Homemade Dough, without Wheat, Barley, or Rye

We are so excited to present our delicious five-minute gluten-free bread recipes. They let us bring a world of bread to people who've gone without for too long. This is the fifth title in our ***Bread in Five Minutes*** cookbook series, based on refrigerating and storing a large quantity of pre-mixed dough (mix once and bake many loaves from the same batch over the next five to ten days). ***Gluten-Free Artisan Bread in Five Minutes a Day*** extends our revolutionary stored-dough method to yeasted breads made without wheat, barley, rye, or any variants of those grains. We've adapted the rich palette of world breads to our unique way of baking, and wherever we could, we converted our readers' favorites from our wheat-bread books into gluten-free versions.

We are a doctor and a pastry chef who met in our kids' music class in 2003—an unlikely place for coauthors to meet. In the swirl of toddlers, musical chairs, and xylophones, there was time for the grown-ups to talk.

Zoë mentioned that she was a pastry chef and baker who'd been trained at the Culinary Institute of America (CIA). What a fortuitous coincidence. Jeff wasn't a food professional at all, but he'd been tinkering for years with an easy, fast method for making homemade bread. He begged her to try a secret recipe he'd been developing.

Our chance meeting led to a book deal with four titles and over a half million copies in print, and we've been writing cookbooks together ever since. Our first book, **The New Artisan Bread in Five Minutes a Day** (now in a 2013 revised edition), created an unlikely team, but it turned out to be a great combination. One reviewer called us "the chemist and the alchemist," though on any given day we reverse roles at will. Our partnership has worked because amateurs find our breads extraordinarily easy to make, yet aficionados find them utterly delicious. Our very different backgrounds help us write recipes that balance health, ease of preparation, and flavor. This book is our latest attempt at that balancing act—for people who don't eat gluten. They want great bread, but they can't find it in their stores—store-bought gluten-free bread costs a fortune, and it tastes terrible.

Our adventures in gluten-free baking all started with our blog, BreadIn5 .com, which lets us keep in touch with readers who have questions or comments, and which, over the years, has also become a place to share new information that we've learned. We've heard funny and emotional stories of families baking together, and people have even written poems about their breads. Our blog space is also a forum for new recipe requests—some of the most common requests have been health related. People started to request gluten-free recipes back in 2008, so we added a gluten-free chapter to our second book, **Healthy Bread in Five Minutes a Day.** We got a tremendous response from our readers—one wrote that "making gluten-free people bread-happy is not that easy, but you guys have done it!" In the years since that book came out, requests have poured in from as far away as Europe,

Asia, and Australia for a whole book of gluten-free recipes, made with the same five-minute method.

So we adapted our five-minute technique and wrote the book for which some of our readers have been clamoring. Our goal for these new recipes was not just to satisfy the cravings of folks who are on a gluten-free diet. We also wanted their friends and loved ones who do eat wheat to be happy with the bread, and for all of them—gluten-eating and non-gluten-eating alike—to be able to eat together. So every recipe had to pass the test of our family members, who are not celiac or gluten-intolerant and love traditional breads. They kept us honest and diligent in our pursuit of fantastic bread that just happens to be made without wheat. Zoë's dad declared the gluten-free brioche to be the best bread he's ever had, not knowing that he was eating something made with rice, tapioca, sorghum, and other gluten-free flours. Zoë knew her two boys would love all the sweets in the book, but when she saw how they finished off gluten-free sandwich breads and dinner rolls, she knew we were onto something. We all know how picky and (painfully) honest kids can be, so this bread had to pass as the real deal for them.

But it wasn't just our loyal family members who were pleased. A fellow food-blogger who taste-tested loaves for us declared them to be "real bread" and said she never would've known they were gluten-free if we hadn't told her. She is one of many who live without bread because she is gluten-intolerant, and her options are so bleak. One reader wrote to say ". . . thank you so much for creating these gluten-free recipes. It's nice to know that even though I can't eat gluten, I can enjoy amazing breads."

And so, with the generous advice of our readers and their families on our interactive website, and after five years of writing and testing gluten-free recipes for our second, third, and fourth books, we've discarded everything that's intimidating and created wonderful gluten-free recipes that come together quickly enough to fit into people's busy lives. Our recipes will let

Visit GFBreadIn5.com, where you'll find recipes, photos, videos, and instructional material.

you create your own homemade gluten-free bread, with the wonderful aroma, flavor, and chewy texture of traditional artisan loaves. We won't ask anyone to knead; it turns out that gluten-free dough never benefits from it. And we've kept active preparation time to five minutes per loaf for the basic recipes, using our usual mix-once bake-many method. There are also two new gluten-free flour blends to keep on hand, so you can dip into the bin whenever you want to mix up a new four-loaf batch—no need to measure from several flour bags every time you mix.

As you read through the book, please visit our website (GFBreadIn5.com), where you'll find instructional text, photographs, videos, and a community of other five-minute-a-day bakers. We're also on Twitter (@ArtisanBreadIn5), Pinterest (Pinterest.com/BreadIn5), Facebook (Facebook.com/BreadIn5), Instagram (Instagram.com/BreadIn5), Tumblr (BreadIn5.Tumblr.com), and Google Plus (Plus.Google.com/+BreadIn5).

Happy baking, and enjoy all the bread!

So what's the problem with gluten? For whom? A wee bit of science:

If you and your health professional have already figured out that you have a problem with gluten, you may not need this section, and if you like, just skip ahead to our discussion of gluten-free and non-gluten-free bread ingredients on page 11.

But if you're just starting the conversation and sorting through competing claims made in the gluten-free community, this next section may be helpful to you.

Americans in record numbers are trying gluten-free foods, and one often-quoted study estimates that 1 out of 133 Americans has celiac disease, and other estimates are as high as one out of a hundred. Indications suggest that the numbers are rising—the U.S. Food and Drug Administration has published an estimate of three million celiacs in the United States. Studies suggest that celiac disease is four times more common today than it was in the 1950s.

But the current state of medical research on gluten-related problems is confusing, even to doctors. When Jeff was in medical school, his adult medicine textbook covered celiac disease in just over one page (in a 2,212-page book). It claimed that there were "insufficient data to provide an accurate estimation" of how common this problem was, which may have been true at the time the book was published (1983). As late as 2000, a popular pediatric textbook claimed that celiac disease was becoming *less* common, and that it affected no more than one in ten thousand people. Off by a factor of a hundred. Well, no one's perfect.

ᖰᖱ

Sometimes you have to admit you just didn't know: Suffice it to say that the most experienced doctors (those who trained in the 1980s and before) were trained to consider celiac disease to be an uncommon problem—most left training believing it was rare. It is not.

A host of studies done over the last decade have helped us to understand how common this problem is. There are three kinds of medical problems caused by eating wheat, barley, rye, and their variants:

(continued)

1. Celiac disease, affecting nearly one out of a hundred people in Western countries (probably over three million Americans), is classified as an "autoimmune" disorder, in which the body's immune system attacks its own healthy tissue. It's part of a family of diseases that includes rheumatoid arthritis, lupus, type 1 diabetes, Crohn's disease, multiple sclerosis, and many others. In autoimmune disorders, the immune system confuses what is foreign (bacteria, viruses, cancer cells) with what is not (our own healthy cells). In celiac disease, the body mounts an immune response triggered by gluten protein—and this immune response attacks healthy cells lining the small intestine. The intestine becomes an innocent bystander in an attack by an immune system that thinks gluten is a deadly invader and has mistaken intestinal cells for it. The result can be a laundry list of unpleasant digestive and other symptoms. The damaged intestine doesn't absorb crucial nutrients very well—nutrients like iron, without which we develop anemia. Though blood tests and symptoms may suggest celiac disease, it is definitively diagnosed only through biopsy of the upper small intestine during endoscopy, performed by a gastrointestinal specialist. There is only one effective treatment—complete avoidance of gluten—and it works. Intestinal healing begins within days of starting a gluten-free diet, but complete healing can take twelve to eighteen months in children, and longer in adults. People with celiac disease can tolerate only the tiniest amounts of gluten—most will have intestinal damage when the amount eaten daily reaches just 100 milligrams ($1/200$ of an ounce), but a recent review suggests that as little as 10 milligrams ($1/2000$ of an ounce) is the threshold for some (not all) celiacs. Most important, celiac disease is *not* an allergy.

2. Wheat allergy: Some people develop particular types of proteins called antibodies in response to foods they eat, and these antibodies inappropriately

(continued)

activate a class of white blood cells—mast cells—that can trigger symptoms which include hives, itching, runny nose, wheezing, swelling of the lips, face, tongue, or throat, nausea, vomiting, and in severe cases, anaphylactic shock (a dangerous decrease in blood pressure). These symptoms occur soon after eating the allergy-triggering food. The most common food allergens are peanuts, tree nuts, shellfish, seafood, eggs, and milk; wheat allergies are much less common. The triggering allergen can be gluten, or other components of the wheat seed. Wheat allergy is typically seen in children, many of whom will also have other food allergies. Kids often outgrow wheat allergy between the ages of three and five, so it's uncommon in adolescents and adults—much less common than celiac disease. But until it disappears, the best treatment is complete avoidance of wheat.

3. Wheat or gluten sensitivity: Research is just beginning to emerge about this newly described syndrome. We're not even close to knowing just how common it is. Why? Because researchers haven't even established clear criteria for its diagnosis. Here's what's known: there are people who experience digestive symptoms on a typical unrestricted diet, but find no traditional medical explanation to account for them—in other words, biopsy results are normal (these people don't have celiac disease). The most recent research suggests that a small but significant group of these people improve when they stop eating wheat. There may be two types, one more similar to celiac disease (but without the intestinal damage), and another that behaves more like an allergy. It appears that *something* is present; we just don't know exactly what.

Expert's Corner: In 2014, we chatted with **Dr. Stefano Guandalini**, medical director of the University of Chicago's Celiac Disease Center, about the growing numbers of Americans who are experimenting with gluten-free foods but *do not* have celiac disease. He agrees that a wheat-sensitivity diagnosis is difficult to pin down, because there's still no scientifically valid medical test to diagnose this condition—no blood or fluid test, no biopsy, and no X-ray. Dr. Guandalini estimates that there are about as many people with gluten/wheat sensitivity or wheat allergy as there are celiacs, which means that about 2 percent of the population has some degree of difficulty with wheat. Making the picture even more complicated, it may not even be gluten that's causing the problem—it may be a different substance in the wheat kernel, such as a carbohydrate or a different protein. Much, much more research is needed before we make blanket pronouncements about any risks of wheat-eating by non-celiacs. Specifically, Dr. Guandalini, who is an international leader in the movement to aggressively identify and diet-treat people with celiac disease, finds no scientific evidence that a gluten-free diet is somehow healthier for everyone. It's clear that people with celiac disease need this diet, and others (we don't know how many) may also benefit by avoiding gluten. But for the rest of the population, there's no reason to believe that there are general health benefits to a gluten-free diet—there is no medical evidence that it will help you lose weight, improve your energy level, or prevent heart disease, dementia, or other chronic conditions.

What do you do if you think you have a problem with gluten?

If you've been diagnosed with celiac disease by a doctor, you need to completely avoid wheat, barley, and rye, but also the lesser-known wheat varieties, even those marketed as "ancient" grains—bulgur, einkorn, spelt, emmer, faro, triticale, *freekeh*, durum, semolina, or Kamut—so you won't find any of those in this book, either. That's because they're actually just older wheat varieties that were used before extensive breeding and hybridization of high-yield wheat occurred in modern agricultural societies, and they still contain gluten (though usually less than modern wheat). On the other hand, there are some "ancient" grains that are *not* wheat varieties, and they are completely gluten-free: quinoa, amaranth, buckwheat, millet, and teff.

Oat flour and oatmeal, in their pure states, *are* gluten-free, but commercial oat products may contain small amounts of gluten because they're sometimes grown or processed in close proximity to wheat. That's why some celiacs should only eat certified gluten-free oats. If you only have wheat sensitivity (see page 7), you should be able to eat commercial oats, but as always, check with your doctor.

௳

Getting tested: The University of Chicago Celiac Disease Center recommends that you wait to start a gluten-free diet until *after* you're diagnosed; otherwise, your test results may be inaccurate. If your diet is already completely gluten-free,

(continued)

Visit GFBreadIn5.com, where you'll find recipes, photos, videos, and instructional material.

your test results will be normal even if you have celiac disease, and they'll remain so for some time after you go back on gluten. If you've already gone gluten-free, ask your doctor how long you need to be back on a regular diet before the testing will be accurate. The Celiac Disease Center has a terrific patient diet guide called **Jump Start Your Gluten-Free Diet**, which offers advice on getting an accurate diagnosis and asking your doctor the right questions (see Sources Consulted, page 275).

"But I just feel better off gluten": What if you've gotten the right tests (while continuing to eat gluten) and the results are still normal, but you still feel better when you avoid wheat, barley, or rye? We'll tell you what Dr. Guandalini has told us: "Don't argue with success." We don't yet understand the science behind every experience, but if eating something made us feel ill, we'd stop eating it, too.

If you don't have celiac disease, but think you may have wheat or gluten sensitivity or allergies, consider an evaluation by a knowledgeable physician. And if you have multiple allergies, check with your doctor before adding anything new to your diet—including ingredients in this book.

So what can I eat? What can't I eat?

What follows are lists of flours and other baking ingredients—first, those that are gluten-free, and second, those that contain gluten, including the most common bread ingredients. Check the websites of the American College of Gastroenterology or the University of Chicago's Celiac Disease Center for more complete lists (see Sources Consulted, page 275). We didn't put so-called "ancient" wheat variants on the gluten-free list—because they *do* contain gluten.

Gluten-Free Flours and Bread-Baking Ingredients

The Center for Celiac Research and Treatment at Massachusetts General Hospital/Harvard Medical School has identified six "super" gluten-free ingredients: amaranth, buckwheat, millet, quinoa, sorghum, and teff (see Sources Consulted, page 275). These "Super Six" provide extremely high "nutrition density." In other words, they contain lots of fiber, vitamins, and minerals in relation to their calorie (energy) content—so we used them wherever we could.

Almond
Amaranth*
Beans and bean flours
Buckwheat*
Corn, cornmeal, and cornstarch
Garbanzo beans and garbanzo flour
Millet*
Nut flours like almond, peanut, walnut
   (though people with multiple allergies
   should be cautious with nuts)
Oats (see notes on certified oats,
   page 9)
Potato

Psyllium
Quinoa*
Rice (white, brown,
   or wild)
Sorghum*
Soy
Tapioca
Teff*
Typical yeast products *that
   don't* contain added
   enzymes; usually will be
   labeled gluten-free

*a Harvard "Super Six"
ingredient

∽

Should I buy products that are specifically labeled gluten-free? Many people with celiac disease are safest with products that the manufacturer has labeled as gluten-free, though others may not need to be so careful. In 2013, the U.S. Food and Drug Administration established limits for how much gluten can be present in foods labeled as gluten-free: 20 parts per million by weight. That means that a pound of gluten-free flour can contain no more than about 3 ten-thousandths of an ounce of gluten. If you've gone metric, then it's about one-fiftieth of a gram per kilogram of food. That is not much. The University of Chicago's Celiac Disease Center says that celiacs will experience intestinal injury at something between 10 and 100 grams per day of gluten ingestion. So if it's labeled "gluten-free" in the United States, even the most sensitive celiacs should be able to eat it. Consult with your doctor if you have any questions.

Flours and Baking Ingredients that Contain Gluten and Cannot Be Eaten by Celiacs or Others Who Cannot Tolerate Gluten or Wheat

Wheat (all-purpose flour, bread flour, whole wheat flour, wheat bran, wheat germ, graham flour, pastry flour)
Barley and barley malt

Bulgur
Durum
Einkorn
Emmer

Faro (sometimes spelled
   farro)
Freekeh
Kamut
Rye
Semolina
Spelt

Sprouted wheat, sprouted
   wheat flour
Triticale
Yeast containing enzymes
   that enhance wheat doughs
   ("dough enhancers");
   the enzymes are often
   derived from wheat

How do you make gluten-free bread in five minutes a day?

Gluten-Free Artisan Bread in Five Minutes a Day is our attempt to help home bakers re-create the great ethnic and American breads of years past using gluten-free ingredients, *without investing serious time in the process.* We've transformed our original recipes into gluten-free creations that will put store-bought gluten-free loaves to shame. Using our straightforward, fast, and easy recipes, anyone will be able to create gluten-free bread and pastry at home with minimal equipment.

How do you make bread without gluten, the protein that gives bread its texture and rise? And who has time to make bread every day?

It turns out that *we* do, and with a method as fast as ours, you can, too. Using xanthan gum or ground psyllium husk to replace the structure that gluten provides, we were able to reproduce our method for storing dough in the refrigerator.

Traditional breads made the old-fashioned way (gluten-free included) need a lot of attention, especially if you want to use a "starter" for that

---

Visit GFBreadIn5.com, where you'll find recipes, photos, videos, and instructional material.

natural, tangy taste. But traditional starters need to be cared for, with water and flour replenished on a schedule—you'll get the flavor without all that work if you bake our way. And traditional bread baking requires lots of cleanup time, especially if you plan to bake frequently. There are bowls and utensils galore to be washed, some of which can't go into the dishwasher. Very few busy people can go through this every day, if ever. Even if your friends are all food fanatics, when was the last time you had homemade bread at a dinner party? What if some of the dinner guests were gluten-free?

So we went to work. We adapted a selection of the great breads we created for **The New Artisan Bread in Five Minutes a Day**, this time using only gluten-free ingredients. Making great homemade gluten-free bread depends on one fortuitous discovery:

Pre-mixed, pre-risen, high-moisture, gluten-free dough keeps well in the refrigerator.

By pre-mixing high-moisture dough and then storing it, daily gluten-free bread baking becomes an easy activity; the only steps you do every day are shaping and baking. Other books have considered refrigerating dough, but only for a few days.

Knead gluten-free dough? Never! Traditional wheat bakers knead dough to develop the gluten, which enhances the structure and rising. Gluten-free dough doesn't require kneading, ever—there's nothing to "develop."

We tested the capacity of wet gluten-free dough to be stored in your refrigerator. As our high-moisture dough ages, it takes on sourdough notes reminiscent of the great European and American natural starters. When dough is mixed with adequate water (this dough will be wetter than most you have worked with), it can be stored in the refrigerator for up to ten days (you can freeze dough that you want to keep longer). That, in a nutshell, is how you make gluten-free breads with only five minutes a day of active effort—the dough is mixed and ready for use in your refrigerator.

Measuring and mixing the dough takes less than fifteen minutes. Kneading, as we've said, is not necessary. Every day, pull off a piece of dough from the container and briefly pat it into shape. Allow it to rest and then toss it in the oven. We don't count the rest time (60 minutes or less depending on the recipe) or baking time (usually about 40 minutes) in our five-minute-a-day calculation, since you can be doing something else while that's happening. The method is so convenient that you probably will find you can portion out some dough and bake a loaf every morning before your day starts (especially if you make flatbreads like pita). **If you want to have one thing you do every day that is simply perfect, this is it.**

Using high-moisture, pre-mixed, pre-risen dough makes most of the difficult, time-consuming, and demanding steps in traditional bread baking completely superfluous:

1. You don't need to mix fresh dough every day to bake a daily gluten-free bread: Stored dough makes wonderful fresh loaves. Only the shaping and baking steps are done daily; the rest has been done in advance.

2. You don't need a "sponge" or "starter": Traditional sourdough recipes require that you keep flour-water mixtures bubbling along in your refrigerator, with careful attention and replenishment. By storing the dough over five to ten days, a subtle sourdough character gradually develops in our breads without the need to maintain sponges or starters in the refrigerator. With our dough-storage approach, your first loaf is not exactly the same as the last. Its flavor will become more complex as the dough ages. Some of our readers learned to stagger their batches so they were always baking with dough that had aged at least a few days—we love that strategy.

3. You don't need to "proof" yeast: Traditional recipes require that yeast be dissolved in water with a little sugar and allowed to sit for five minutes to prove that bubbles can form and the yeast is alive. But modern yeast

What We *Don't* Have to Do: Steps from Traditional Artisan Baking That We Omitted

1. Mix a new batch of dough every time we want to make bread.

2. "Proof" yeast.

3. Knead dough: Kneading develops gluten, which these breads don't have!

4. Rest and rise the loaves in a draft-free location—it doesn't matter.

5. Fuss over doubling or tripling of dough volume.

6. Punch down and re-rise: **Never** punch down stored dough.

7. Poke rising loaves, leaving indentations to be sure they've "proofed."

Now you know why it only takes five minutes a day, not including resting and baking time.

simply doesn't fail if used before its expiration date and the baker re-members to use lukewarm, *not hot* water. The high water content in our doughs further ensures that the yeast will fully hydrate and activate with-out a proofing step. Storage gives it plenty of time to ferment the dough—our approach doesn't need the head start.

4. It's hard to over-rise high-moisture stored dough: Remember that you're storing it anyway. Assum-ing you start with lukewarm (not cold) water, you'll see a brisk initial rise at room temperature over two hours (don't punch down); then the risen dough is refrigerated for use over the next five to ten days. But rising longer (even as long as eight hours) won't be harmful; there's lots of leeway in the initial rise time. The exception is dough made with eggs or dairy, which should complete its rising in the refrigerator if it goes be-yond two hours.

Given these simple principles, anyone can make gluten-free bread at home. We'll talk about what you'll need in Chapters 2 (Ingredients) and 3 (Equipment). You don't need a professional baker's kitchen. In Chapter 4, you'll learn the tips and techniques that have taken us years to accumulate. Then, in Chapters 5 and 6 (The Flour Mixtures and The Master Recipe, respectively), we'll lay out the basics of our method, applying them to a basic round loaf and several delicious variations. The Master Recipe in Chapter 6 is the model for the rest of our recipes. We suggest you read it carefully and bake it first before trying anything else. You won't regret it. And if you want more information, we're on the Web at GFBreadIn5.com, where you'll find instructional text, photographs, videos, and a community of other five-minute bakers. Other easy ways to keep in touch: follow us on Twitter (@ArtisanBreadin5), on Facebook (Facebook.com/BreadIn5), on Pinterest (Pinterest.com/BreadIn5), on Tumblr (BreadIn5.Tumblr.com), on Google Plus (Plus.Google.com/+BreadIn5), or on our YouTube channel (YouTube.com/BreadIn5), or on Instagram (Instagram.com/BreadIn5).

Visit GFBreadIn5.com, where you'll find recipes, photos, videos, and instructional material.

2

INGREDIENTS

Here's a practical guide to the ingredients we use to produce artisan loaves without wheat, barley, rye, or other ingredients containing gluten. Working with gluten-free flours and doughs, we learned that a blend of gluten-free flours works better than a single flour, and that you need xanthan gum or ground psyllium husk to give gas-trapping structure to the dough. We chose Bob's Red Mill gluten-free baking products for our testing. They gave us great results, and they're available in most U.S. supermarkets, in either the regular baking section or the health food area.

Gluten-Free Flours and Grains

Rice flours: Rice is one of the world's great food staples—all the cultures of the Far East depended on its cultivation to develop their civilizations. Brown or white rice flour can be interchanged, cup for cup, in our all-purpose gluten-free flour mixture (page 61), though you may need to add a little extra water if you use brown rice flour. Retaining the external bran and germ, brown rice flour is much higher in nutrients and fiber than white rice flour, but white rice flour makes loaves with finer texture and cleaner flavor. Avoid rice flours labeled as "glutinous"—those have different baking properties (though in this case "glutinous" has nothing to do with wheat gluten). And when using white rice flour, we avoided Asian food market products, which were highly variable in how much water they absorbed—we tested instead with Bob's Red Mill "Stone Ground White Rice Flour" (not "Sweet Rice Flour").

Tapioca flour/Tapioca starch: Tapioca is made from a root that's known by many names: cassava, manioc, or yuca. It is extracted and ground into a flour that is high in starch, calcium, and vitamin C, but low in protein. It is most often used for its thickening properties, but it now frequently appears in gluten-free baking. It is sold as both tapioca flour and starch, and the most popular product has both of those names on the label. Unlike potato starch (see page 21) and potato flour (see page 21), they are exactly the same.

Sorghum: Sorghum is a cooking grain related to sugarcane. It's popular the world around, but it has only recently found its way into North American kitchens. The flour made from its seeds is high in nutrition and has a slightly sweet, nutty flavor that works well in whole-grain recipes.

Cornmeal and Cornstarch: Cornmeal is just the whole dehulled corn kernel, ground coarsely into a "meal"; it makes a great base for sliding loaves off a peel. Degerminated cornmeal has had its nutritious "germ" removed, but it has better shelf life at room temperature, so many commercial cornmeals are sold that way. When used in dough, it gives great crunch and character to gluten-free breads. Cornstarch is a different animal—it's a refined product that has neither the bran nor the germ—just the starch. It creates a smooth texture and acts as a binder in gluten-free dough.

Oats: Raw oats or oat flour adds a wonderful hearty flavor and contribute a toothsome texture to bread. As they grow from the ground, oats are gluten-free, but they can only be certified as such if they are milled in a gluten-free facility; typical commercial oats may have traces of gluten because oats are often grown or processed in close proximity to wheat. Consider buying products labeled gluten-free if you can't tolerate gluten at all.

Organic flours: We don't detect flavor or texture differences with organic gluten-free flours, but if you like organic products, by all means use them. They're not required, they certainly cost more, and they aren't always available.

Potato starch: The starch from potatoes captures moisture in baked gluten-free products, so it's a small but important component in Flour Mixture #1 (page 60). Potato flour performs differently, and it can't be substituted.

Millet flour: Millet is the primary ingredient in (of all things!) bird seed, but it's a major food staple in Africa. Turns out it's one of nature's perfect foods, and (ground) millet flour worked beautifully as a substitute for barley in our Moroccan *Ksra* bread (page 203). When used unground as whole seeds, it adds great texture to our 100% Whole-Grain Loaf (page 102).

Teff flour: An indispensable grain in Ethiopia, teff had been virtually unheard of in the rest of the world until recently. It is a variety of whole-grain millet that is wonderfully sweet and packed with iron and calcium. When combined with caraway seeds, it's a dead ringer for a traditional German or Eastern European rye loaf.

Visit GFBreadIn5.com, where you'll find recipes, photos, videos, and instructional material.

Xanthan gum: This powdered additive, a naturally derived gum that creates gas-trapping structure in dough, is used in gluten-free breads to replace the resiliency and chew that wheat breads get from gluten.

Ground Psyllium Husk: This product, milled from the outer coating of an edible seed, is a natural fiber supplement that creates structure in gluten-free dough. It works well as a substitute for xanthan gum (though you need to adjust the amount in some recipes). Ground psyllium husk is available at your local pharmacy, food coop, or online, sometimes sold as "powdered" psyllium husk.

Guar gum: We've found that guar gum doesn't create enough structure to be used in our stored gluten-free dough. In our method, you need to trap gas *and* store dough long-term in the refrigerator, and that requires more structure than guar gum creates.

Commercial gluten-free flour blends: There are a number of commercial gluten-free flour blends on the market today, and more will be appearing in the years to come. Some of the products may be able to be swapped for Mixture #1 (Gluten-Free All-Purpose Flour on page 60), but you may need to add xanthan gum or psyllium to the mixture, up to 1½ teaspoons per 6 cups of flour, if the mixture doesn't already have it. In any case, it'll take some trial and error—start with a small batch.

Water

Throughout the book we call for lukewarm water. This means water that feels just a little warm to the touch; if you measured it with a thermometer it would be no higher than 100°F (38°C). The truth is, we never use a thermometer, and we've never had a yeast failure due to excessive temperature—but it can happen, so be careful.

About water sources: We find that the flavors of grain and yeast overwhelm the contribution of water to bread's flavor. We use ordinary tap water run through a home water filter, but that's only because it's what we drink at home. Assuming your own tap water tastes good enough to drink, use it filtered or unfiltered; we can't tell the difference in finished bread.

Yeast

Our approach works with all the national brands of yeast (though we tested our recipes with the Red Star brand), and you can use packages labeled "granulated," "active dry," "instant," "quick-rise," or "bread-machine." **Be sure that the yeast you choose does not include wheat-derived dough enhancers.** Most yeast products don't have them and will be labeled as gluten-free. Fresh cake yeast works fine as well (though you will have to increase the yeast volume by 50 percent to achieve the same rising speed). The long storage time of our doughs acts as an equalizer between all of those subtly different yeast products. **One strong**

Using yeast packets instead of jarred or bulk yeast: Throughout the book, we call for 1 tablespoon of granulated yeast for about 4 pounds of dough. **You can substitute 1 packet of granulated yeast for 1 tablespoon, even though, technically speaking, those amounts aren't perfectly equivalent (1 tablespoon is a little more than the 2¼ teaspoons found in one packet).** We've found that this makes little difference in the initial rise time or in the performance of the finished dough.

Visit GFBreadIn5.com, where you'll find recipes, photos, videos, and instructional material.

recommendation: **If you bake frequently, buy yeast in bulk or in 4-ounce jars, rather than in packets, which are much less economical.**

Food co-ops often sell yeast by the pound, in bulk (usually the Red Star brand). Make sure that bulk-purchased yeast is fresh and gluten-free by chatting with your co-op manager. Freeze yeast after opening to extend its shelf life, and use it straight from the freezer, or store smaller containers in the refrigerator and use within a few months. Between the two of us, we've had only one yeast failure in many years of baking, and it was with an out-dated envelope stored at room temperature. **The real key to avoiding yeast failure is to use water that is no warmer than lukewarm (about 100°F). Hot water kills yeast.**

Modern Yeast . . .

. . . almost never fails if used before its expiration date, so you *do not* need to "proof" the yeast (i.e., test it for freshness by demonstrating that it bubbles in sweetened warm water). And you don't have to wait for yeast to fully dissolve after mixing with water. In fact, in this book, we mix all the dry ingredients first, and **then** add liquids.

After several days of high-moisture storage, yeasted dough begins to take on a flavor and aroma that's close to the flavor of natural sourdough starters used in many artisan breads. This will deepen the flavor and character of all your doughs. The traditional way to achieve these flavors—pre-ferments, sours, and

(continued)

starters like *biga* (Italian), *levain* (French), and *poolish* (Eastern European)—all require significant time and attention. Our method provides the flavor without all that effort.

Salt: Adjust It to Your Taste

Salt adds flavor and attracts and holds moisture in baked bread. All of our recipes were tested with Morton brand kosher salt, which is coarsely ground. If you measure salt by volume and you're using something finer or coarser, you need to adjust the amount because finer salt packs denser in the spoon. The following measurements are equivalent:

Weighing yeast and salt: In the dough recipes, we provide weight equivalents for yeast and salt, which is a more professional technique—but professionals measure out enormous batches. Be sure your home scale weighs accurately in the lower ranges; otherwise, spoon-measure yeast and salt.

- **Table salt (fine):** 2 teaspoons
- **Morton Coarse Kosher Salt (coarse):** 1 tablespoon
- **Diamond Crystal Kosher Salt (coarsest):** 1 tablespoon plus 1 teaspoon

You can use sea salt, but be sure to adjust for its grind. If it's finely ground, you need to measure it like table salt above, and if it's more coarsely ground than Morton, you'll need to increase the volume accordingly. And reserve the really expensive artisan sea salts for sprinkling on finished products—artisan salts lose their unique flavors when baked. **If you decide to weigh salt to avoid the problem of compensating for fineness-of-grind, do so only for double batches or larger unless you're really confident of your scale's performance at low weights (see page 25).**

Adjust the salt to suit your palate and your health—we give you a range. We love the taste of salt and don't have any health-related salt restrictions, so we tend to use the higher amounts. Saltier dough can help bring out flavor early in the batch life, but if you like our doughs best after they've been stored awhile, you may find you can decrease the salt. The low end of our salt range will be salty enough for many—and if health conditions require it, you can decrease the salt radically and the recipes will still work. In fact, you can bring the salt all the way down to zero, though the taste will certainly change.

Seeds and Nuts

Many of our testers found that seeds of all sorts improved their gluten-free breads and flatbreads. Caraway seeds are so central to the flavor of ordinary rye bread (*with* gluten) that a lot of people thought that our gluten-free breads made with caraway were true rye—they were not. (Rye contains gluten and isn't used in this book.) Other seeds and nuts work great too, so experiment with sesame seeds, poppy seeds, and nuts—you can add them to any recipe you like. The oil inside seeds or nuts can go rancid if you keep them too long. Taste a few if your jar is older than a year, and freeze them if you are storing for longer than three months.

Nut Flours

Almond flour: Whole almonds are ground into a fine flour, which is also called almond meal. It is high in protein and low in carbohydrates. You can use either blanched or raw almond meal. Store in the freezer to prevent the oils in the nuts from going rancid.

Coconut flour: It's just dehydrated coconut, ground into a powder. It has the natural sweetness and richness of coconut and is high in fiber and protein.

Chocolate

Some of our enriched breads call for chocolate, either cocoa powder, bar chocolate, or chunks. Use the highest-quality chocolate if you can—it improves the flavor. For cocoa powder, it doesn't matter if it's labeled "Dutch-process" (alkali-treated) or not. The question of Dutch process is only important for baked goods risen with baking soda or baking powder—yeast doesn't seem to care. If premium chocolate isn't available, try the recipes with your favorite supermarket brands.

Sweeteners

Agave syrup: Agave syrup, sometimes labeled "agave nectar," tastes the tiniest bit like tequila, and no wonder. The agave plant is the source of the fermentable juice that makes the world's best tequila, and agave syrup is the concentrated sweetener made from that juice. You can substitute it for honey or maple syrup if you prefer the flavor in recipes calling for those natural sweeteners.

Honey: This is the sweetener we call for in our brioche and challah, produced by busy bees the world over from naturally occurring sugars in the nectar of the flowers that they visit. Honey's flavor is determined by the type of plant nectar the honeybee collects. Some honeys have very intense flavor, such as buckwheat honey, while others are quite mild, like clover honey. We've had nice results with all kinds of honey, so experiment with different types and see which you prefer.

Maple syrup: The most commonly found maple syrup is Grade A, which is lightest in color and mildest in flavor. Many consider it the more desirable grade, but we actually prefer to use Grade B, which is made later in the production season and has a darker color, stronger flavor, and more of the minerals magnesium and zinc. It is great for baking because the flavor stands up to the other ingredients, but either Grade A or B will work nicely.

Molasses: Molasses is an unrefined sweetener derived from sugarcane. Blackstrap molasses is the product of three boilings of the sugarcane, and so it concentrates the nutrients. Its iron, magnesium, calcium, copper, potassium, and vitamin B_6 content makes it one of the most nutrient-rich sweeteners, more so than molasses that isn't labeled as blackstrap (though you can use any kind in the recipes). It adds color and a deep, rich flavor.

⁓

Can I use stevia in place of sugar or other sugar-containing sweeteners? Some readers have asked us about this herbal sweetener—stevia sweetens without sugar. But it's not an artificial sweetener, it's an extract of a South American herb whose leaves contain a naturally occurring, zero-calorie substance that is much sweeter than sugar. There are two kinds of stevia products: pure ones (liquid or powder), and those combined with other substances—starch or sugar-derived additives like erythritol or maltodextrin—so that the resulting product measures and looks like granulated sugar. If you use the pure stevia products, you only use a small amount—it has much more concentrated sweetening power. The labeling will tell you the volume equivalency with other sweeteners. You can experiment with stevia in place of sugar, honey, or other sweeteners in any of our recipes. It doesn't taste exactly the same, and you'll have to experiment with the amount of liquid in the recipe, but many people find it to be a natural product that makes a nice substitute. But note that it doesn't increase browning the way regular sweeteners do.

3

EQUIPMENT

In the spirit of our approach, we've tried to keep our list spare and present items in order of importance. The most helpful items are:

- Equipment for baking with steam: we'll give you four options
- Baking stone, cast-iron pizza pan, cast-iron skillet, or unglazed quarry tiles
- Oven thermometer
- Pizza peel

See Sources for Bread-Baking Products (page 274) to locate mail-order and Web-based vendors for harder-to-find items.

Equipment for Baking with Steam (You Only Need One of These)

Metal broiler tray to hold boiling water for steam: This is our first choice for creating the steam needed for lean-dough breads—those made without much fat or eggs—to achieve a crispy crust. (Enriched breads like challah and brioche don't benefit from baking with steam because the fat in the

❀

Two important warnings: 1. Do not use a glass pan to catch water for steam, or it will shatter on contact with the water. 2. We've even gotten rare reports of cracked oven-window glass from accidentally spilled water. If you want extra assurance that this won't happen, cover the window with a towel before pouring water into the tray; remove before closing the oven door.

dough softens the crust.) Pour hot water (or drop a handful of ice cubes) into the preheated broiler tray just before closing the oven door.

Some ovens (including most professional-style ones and many that heat with gas) don't have a good seal for holding in steam. *If your oven allows steam to dissipate and you're not getting a beautiful crust with the broiler-tray method, try one of these three alternatives:*

1. **Food-grade water sprayer:** Spray the loaf with water

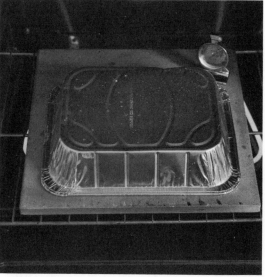

before closing the oven door, then open it at thirty-second intervals for two more sprayings.

2. Metal bowl or aluminum-foil roasting pan for covering free-form loaves in the oven: By trapping steam next to the loaf as it bakes, you can create the humid environment that produces a crisp crust without using a broiler tray or a sprayer. The bowl or dish needs to be heat tolerant and tall enough so that the rising loaf won't touch it, but not so large that it hangs beyond the edge of the stone, or it won't trap the steam. Remove for the last third of the baking time.

3. Bake inside a clay baker or a covered cast-iron pot: The clay baker (in French, *la cloche* [la klōsh], meaning "bell," after its distinctive shape) is a time-honored way to bake—the covered baking vessel traps steam inside, so the crackling crust forms without the need for a baking stone, broiler tray, water, or sprayer. Crispiest results are obtained with a twenty- to thirty-minute preheat. We don't soak clay bakers in water before use as is sometimes ad-

vocated, and unglazed clay shouldn't be greased. It's easiest to rest the loaf on parchment paper, and then carefully slide the loaf, paper and all, into the preheated baker when ready to bake. Start the baking with the cover on, but finish baking *uncovered* for the last third of the baking time. **Covered cast-iron pots (Dutch ovens) also** work well when used this same way, though some of them will need a heat-resistant replacement knob—check with the manufacturer.

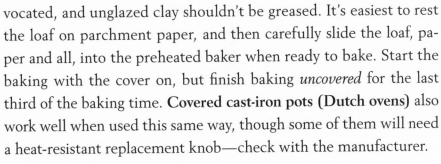

Visit GFBreadIn5.com, where you'll find recipes, photos, videos, and instructional material.

Other Equipment

Baking stone, cast-iron pizza pan, cast-iron skillet, baking steel, or unglazed quarry tiles: Bread turns out browner, crisper, and tastier when the dough

is baked on one of these, especially in combination with steam (page 31). Products may be labeled "pizza stones" (usually round), or "baking stones" (usually rectangular), but they're both made from the same kinds of materials (some kind of ceramic) and perform the same way. The larger ones will keep flour, cornmeal, and other ingredients from falling to the oven floor (we like the 14 x 16-inch models). In our experience, ceramic stones don't last forever. Most are pretty durable, but we no longer find any manufacturers willing to guarantee them against cracking. Thick stones take longer to preheat compared to thin ceramic ones, cast iron or steel (see below). The thick stones are more durable than thin ones, and cast iron or steel are the most durable of all (we haven't heard of those cracking).

Unglazed quarry tiles, available from home-improvement stores, are inexpensive and work well. The drawbacks: You'll need several of them to line an oven shelf, and stray cornmeal or flour may fall between the tiles onto the oven floor, where it will burn.

Traditionally, professionals have given two reasons to bake right on a ceramic stone. **First,** the stone promotes fast and even heat transfer because of its weight and density (versus, for example, a baking sheet), so it quickly dries and crisps the crust. That massive heat transfer also creates "oven spring," especially in home ovens that don't deliver even heat. (Oven spring is the sudden expansion of gasses within the bread—it occurs upon contact with the hot air and stone, and it prevents a dense result.) **Second,** it's always been assumed that the stone's porosity allows it to absorb excess moisture from the dough (especially wet dough), encouraging crispness. It turns out that the effect must be mostly due to explanation number one, because we've found that dough baked on preheated cast-iron pizza pans, and even in preheated cast-iron skillets or baking steels, turns out as well as dough baked on stones, despite the fact that cast iron isn't porous at all.

Having said all this, we must emphasize that you can make decent bread without a baking stone; just bake directly on a heavy-gauge baking sheet (see page 37). The crust won't be as crisp, but the result will be better than any gluten-free bread you can buy. And the oven preheat can be as short as five minutes.

Oven thermometer: Home ovens, even those with digital readouts, are often off by up to 75 degrees, so this is an important item. You need to know the actual oven temperature to get predictable bread-baking results. An inexpensive oven thermometer (less than twenty dollars) will help you get results like the ones you see in our pictures. Place your oven thermometer right on the baking surface for the most accurate reading.

A hot oven drives excess water out of wet dough, but if it's too hot, you'll burn the crust before fully baking the crumb (the bread's interior). Too low, and you'll end up with a pale crust and undercooked crumb unless you extend the baking time—but that can give you a thick crust. Without the thermometer, your bread baking will have an annoying element of trial and error. If your oven runs significantly hot or cool, you may want to have it recalibrated by a professional. Otherwise, just compensate by adjusting your heat setting.

When a baking stone is in place, your oven may take longer to reach final temperature than the twenty- or thirty-minute preheat that we specify. If you

don't like the result you're getting with a thirty-minute preheat, consider a longer one (forty-five or even sixty minutes).

Pizza peel: This is a flat board with a long handle used to slide bread or pizza onto a hot stone. Wood or metal works well, but you can't use anything made of plastic to transfer dough onto a stone—it could melt upon contact. Prepare the peel with cornmeal or parchment paper before putting dough on it, or everything will stick to it, and possibly to your stone. If you don't have a pizza peel, a rimless baking sheet will do, but it will be more difficult to handle. A wood cutting board also works in a pinch—some have handles that make them almost as easy to work with as peels.

A bucket, large plastic storage container, or a glass, stainless-steel, or crockery container with a lid: You can mix and store the dough in the same vessel—this will save you from washing one more item (it all figures into the five minutes a day). Stand mixers come with handy 5- or 6-quart bowls (4½ quart will work in a pinch), and you can purchase vented plastic lids

for them. Or, look for a food-grade container that holds 5 to 6 quarts, to allow for the initial rise. The same containers can be used to store our flour mixtures (see Chapter 5, pages 60–62). If you're not using a mixer, round containers are easier to mix in than square ones (flour gets caught in corners). Great options are available on our website, or from Tupperware, King Arthur Flour's website, and kitchen-supply specialty stores, as well as discount chains like Costco and Target. Some food-storage buckets include a vented lid, which allows gasses to escape during the fermentation process. You can usually close the vent (or seal the lid) after the first two days, because gas production has really slowed by then. If your vessel has a plastic lid, you can poke a tiny hole in the lid to allow gas to escape. Avoid glass or crockery containers that create a truly airtight seal (with a screw top, for example) because trapped gasses could shatter them. If you don't have a vented container, just leave the lid open a crack for the first two days of storage.

And of course, you can always use a mixing bowl covered with plastic wrap. Don't use a towel—it sticks miserably to high-moisture dough.

Dough scraper ("bench knife"): The dough scraper makes it easier to work with wet dough—especially when you're just starting out. It can help lessen the temptation to work in extra flour to prevent things from sticking to the work surface. Just scrape wet dough off the work surface when it sticks—this is particularly useful when working with dough as it's rolled out for pizza or flatbread. The scraper is also handy for scraping excess cornmeal or flour off your hot baking stone. We 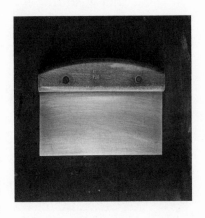 prefer the rigid steel scrapers over the flexible plastic ones—in part because you can't use plastic to scrape off a hot stone.

Heavy-gauge baking sheets, jelly-roll pans, and cookie sheets: The highest-quality baking sheets are made of super-heavyweight aluminum and have short rims (they're sometimes called jelly-roll pans). When well greased or lined with parchment paper or a silicone mat, they are a decent alternative to the pizza peel/baking stone method and let you avoid sliding dough off a pizza peel onto a stone.

Similar-gauge flat, round pans are available specifically for pizza. Avoid "air-insulated" baking sheets—they don't conduct heat well and won't produce a crisp crust. Thin cookie sheets can be used, but like air-insulated bakeware, they won't produce a great crust and can scorch bottom crusts due to their uneven heat delivery.

Silicone mats: They're nonstick, flexible, reusable thousands of times, and some brands will tolerate temperatures of up to 475°F, so they'll work for all the recipes except our high-temperature pizzas (check the labeling for maximum temperature before you buy). Shape the loaf on the mat, and then just drop it on top of a baking sheet, a hot stone, or right on the oven rack. They don't need to be greased, so cleanup is a breeze. Silicone mats are also great for rolling out our wet gluten-free doughs in recipes that call for flattening it thin (or use an oiled piece of parchment paper).

Parchment paper: Use parchment paper that's temperature-rated to withstand what's called for in the recipe. The paper slides off the pizza peel, right onto the preheated stone along with the loaf. It can be removed halfway through baking to crisp up the bottom crust. Parchment paper can also be used to line baking sheets, and this can substitute for greasing the sheet. Don't use products labeled as pastry parchment—they will stick to baked bread dough. And never use wax paper, which will melt.

Baguette pan (metal or silicone): Gluten-free dough is less structured than wheat flour dough, so a baguette pan is especially helpful to prevent the sideways spreading that makes baguettes look, well, homemade. Metal or silicone perforated baguette pans both work nicely—the perforations allow hot air to reach the bottom crust. They are a great way to bake several beautifully shaped baguettes at once, without crowding. If using the metal version of these, cut a sheet of parchment paper to fit, which prevents sticking.

Loaf pans: For sandwich loaves, we prefer the smaller pans with approximate dimensions of 8½ x 4½ inches. This size pan is often labeled as holding one pound of dough, but we specify a more generous fill—up to two pounds when filled about three-quarters full.

Like baking sheets and silicone mats, loaf pans work well but don't promote the development of a crisp and beautifully colored crust—wherever the pan touches the bread, it may be pale compared to free-form loaves. One word of caution about loaf pans: when you're starting out with our wet doughs, use a pan with a nonstick coating, and even then, grease it. Traditional loaf pans (without the nonstick coating) are more challenging. We've had the best success getting loaves to release from traditional uncoated pans when they're made from heavy-gauge aluminum or glazed ceramic—the thin ones don't do as well. Be sure to grease them well with butter or oil.

Mini loaf pans: For smaller sandwich breads, and especially when baking with kids, it's fun to use mini loaf pans—and they have the added benefit of being easier to bake through to the center. They're sometimes labeled "number-1" loaf pans, measure about 6 x 3 inches, and hold about three-quarters of a pound of dough. The loaves bake faster than those in full-size loaf pans, so check for doneness sooner than the recipe calls for when using them.

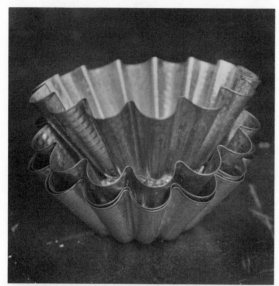

Brioche pans: Traditionally, brioche is baked either in a fluted brioche mold or in a loaf pan. The fluted mold is easy to find either online or in any baking supply store. They are available in several sizes, with or without a nonstick coating. Flexible silicone brioche molds are now also available.

Banneton/brotform: Wicker rising baskets (French = *banneton*, German = *brotform*) have long been favored by artisan bakers for the beautiful flour patterns they impart to the loaves, but we also found they are a great way to keep our very soft doughs from spreading sideways while the loaves are rising. Smaller ones, preferably designed for one or one-and-a-half pounds of dough, are the easiest to work with.

Panettone molds: Large ceramic ramekins or ordinary fluted brioche pans work nicely, or you can buy an authentic panettone pan or panettone molds made from paper.

Dough whisk: Unlike flimsy egg-beating whisks, Danish-style dough whisks are made from strong nonbendable wire on a wood handle, and they're used to blend liquid and dry ingredients together quickly in the dough bucket. We find that they work faster and offer less resistance than a traditional wooden spoon—though a wooden spoon works fine. They also work beautifully to blend our flour mixtures before shaking (see pages 60–62).

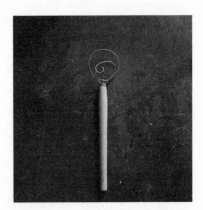

Rolling pin: We love the skinny French rolling pins that look like large dowels, tapered or straight, but traditional American-style pins with handles work well, too. We have tried them all and have determined that wood, marble, and metal all get the job done; we've even rolled out dough with a bottle of wine in a pinch.

Bread knife: A serrated bread knife does a great job cutting through fresh bread without tearing or compressing it. It's the best implement we've found for slashing high-moisture loaves just before baking. Razor blades and French *lames* (lămm), usually recommended in traditional artisan baking, catch and stick in very wet gluten-free dough—not so for serrated bread knives.

Cooling rack: These are fashioned of wire or other thin metal and are usually intended for cake. They are very helpful in preventing the soggy bottom crust that can result when you cool bread on a plate or other nonporous surface.

Measuring cups: Be sure to use **dry** measuring cups for flour, which allow you to level the top of the cup by sweeping across with a knife; you can't level off a liquid measuring cup filled with flour.

Measuring spoons: Seek out a set that includes a ½-tablespoon measure in addition to the usual suspects. Some of our ingredient lists call for ½ tablespoon. If you can't find a measuring spoon set with a ½-tablespoon measure, just measure out 1½ teaspoons.

Scale: We love to weigh our ingredients rather than use measuring cups. It's faster and more accurate, and it has begun to catch on in the United States. Luckily, digital scales are getting cheaper all the time, so we now include weights for ingredients in all our dough recipes. Just press "tare" or "zero" after each ingredient is added to the dough vessel, and you can use these scales without slowing down to do the arithmetic.

The scale is also a consistent way to measure out dough for loaves or flatbreads, but it isn't absolutely necessary because we also give you a visual cue for dough weight (for example, a grapefruit-size piece is one pound, and an orange-size piece is about half a pound of dough).

Stand mixers: Our gluten-free doughs come together more quickly and easily in a stand mixer, though it's definitely not required. But if you're finding your doughs are lumpy, or the baked loaves are denser than you'd like, the stand mixer can help, and this is especially true of our enriched doughs in Chapter 9. Use your machine's paddle attachment (some manufacturers call this a "flat beater"), not the dough hook, which doesn't work well with dough this wet. Start on slow speed to avoid spilling, then increase to medium-high until very smooth and without lumps. A hand mixer will also work, but not as well as a stand mixer.

Pastry brushes: These are used to paint water, oil, or egg onto the surface of the loaf just before baking. We both prefer the natural-bristle style to silicone, but that's a matter of taste.

Plastic wrap: Heavy-duty plastic wrap is great for loosely covering resting loaves or dough containers and also as a top sheet for rolling out thin sheets of dough.

Microplane zester: Microplane zesters are used for removing the zest from citrus fruit without including much of the bitter pith. We use them when we want an assertive citrus flavor that you can't get from the fruit's juice.

Convection ovens: These produce a first-rate brown and crispy crust and speed the baking by circulating hot air. Some older convection models specify that temperatures should be lowered 25 degrees to prevent over-browning, while many recent models make the correction automatically, so check your manual. In some, you'll need to turn the loaf around at the half-way point so that each side will brown evenly. Ignore convection-oven instructions that claim you can skip the preheat—the preheat is necessary for our method, especially if you're using a baking stone. As always, use an oven thermometer to check temperature; air circulation in convection ovens can "fool" thermostats in some ovens, sometimes driving the temperature up as much as 75 degrees.

These instructions apply only to range-based convection ovens, not microwaves with convection modes, which we have not tested.

Visit GFBreadIn5.com, where you'll find recipes, photos, videos, and instructional material.

4

TIPS AND TECHNIQUES

T his chapter will help you perfect your stored-dough gluten-free
breads. In the discussion that follows, we provide tips and techniques
to create breads with a professional-quality crust (exterior) and crumb
(interior).

Measuring Ingredients by Weight

Many readers of our wheat-based bread books, especially those outside the
United States, asked us for weight equivalents, and we've found that weights
are especially helpful for gluten-free flours. Why?
Gluten-free flours are powdery, which makes them
somewhat unpredictable to measure. If you do measure by U.S. volumes (cup measures), be sure to pack
the flour into the cup (as though you were measuring
brown sugar), because that's the way we tested recipes
for this book. Since different people can measure differently, some of our testers appreciated the reliability
of weighing the flours.

Though most American home bakers don't yet weigh their ingredients, weighing is probably the quickest way to mix up a batch of dough—and based on current trends, it may become standard here. So this book has weight equivalents for all dough recipes.

Using digital scales (see Equipment, page 42): Inexpensive digital scales are a snap to use. Simply press the "tare" (zeroing) button after placing your empty mixing vessel on the scale, and weigh your first ingredient. Then tare again before adding each subsequent ingredient. There's less cleanup, and your measurements won't be affected by different scooping styles, or how tightly or loosely compacted your flour was in its bin.

Weighing small-quantity ingredients: Our recipes only require a fraction of an ounce of some ingredients (like salt and yeast). Since many scales for home use are accurate only to the nearest eighth of an ounce (three or four grams), measuring small amounts this way can introduce inaccuracy—this becomes less important when measuring larger quantities for doubled recipes. **Unless you're confident of your scale's accuracy for very small amounts, or you're making a double batch or larger, measure salt and yeast with measuring spoons.**

Measuring Gluten-Free Flours with Cup-Measures

Gluten-free flours tend to be very finely ground, and we've found that using measuring cups can cause measurements to vary, depending on user technique. Weighing the flours takes care of that, but if you want to use cup-measures, **be sure to pack the flour tightly into the cup, like brown sugar**.

Storing Dough to Develop Flavor

All of our recipes are based on dough that can be stored for up to ten days in the refrigerator. That makes our method incredibly convenient. But there's another benefit to storing the dough: Sourdough flavor develops over the life span of the batch. That means that your first loaves won't taste the same as your last ones. Some of our readers have taken to mixing staggered batches, so they're never baking with brand-new dough.

How much to make and store: In order to have fresh-baked artisan bread in only five minutes a day of active preparation time, you'll want to make enough dough to last ten days. Your initial time investment (mixing the dough) is the most significant one, though it generally takes no more than fifteen minutes. By mixing a large batch, you are spreading that investment over more days of bread making. For larger households, that might mean doubling or even tripling the recipes. Don't forget to choose a container large enough to accommodate the rising of the larger batch.

Conversion Tables for Common Liquid Measures

VOLUMES

U.S. Spoon and Cup Measures	U.S. Liquid Volume	Metric Volume
1 teaspoon	$1/6$ ounce	5 ml
1 tablespoon	$1/2$ ounce	15 ml
$1/4$ cup	2 ounces	60 ml
$1/2$ cup	4 ounces	120 ml
1 cup	8 ounces	240 ml
2 cups	16 ounces	475 ml
4 cups	32 ounces	950 ml

OVEN TEMPERATURE: FAHRENHEIT TO CELSIUS CONVERSION

Degrees Fahrenheit	Degrees Celsius
350	180
375	190
400	200
425	220
450	230
475	240
500	250
550	288

Dough Consistency: How Wet Is Wet Enough?

Unfortunately, the gluten-free flour industry is not yet fully standardized, so you may need to adjust the liquid amounts in our recipes. If you find that your doughs are too stiff, decrease the flour by ⅛ cup at a time in subsequent batches (or increase the water by a tablespoon). If they're too loose and wet and don't hold a shape well for free-form loaves, increase the flour, again by ⅛ cup at a time. If you don't want to wait until your next batch to correct a problem with moisture content, you can work extra flour into a too-wet batch (give it some time to absorb after doing this).

Resting and Baking Times Are Approximate

All of our resting and baking times are approximate. Since loaves are formed by hand, their size will vary from loaf to loaf, which means their resting and baking time requirements will vary as well. In general, flat or skinny loaves don't need much resting time and will bake rapidly. Large, high-domed loaves require longer resting and baking times. So unless you're weighing out exact one-pound loaves and forming the same shapes each time, your resting and baking times may vary, and our listed times should be seen only as a starting point.

A 60-minute rest will give you a nice crumb structure. Skinny loaves (like baguettes, see page 75) or flatbreads (see Chapter 8) do well with short resting times; in fact, pizza and many flatbreads need none at all.

Preparing the Pizza Peel—Gluten-Free Grains or Parchment Paper?

Many of our recipes call for sliding the loaf off a pizza peel directly onto a hot baking stone. Parchment paper keeps the oven cleanest, but cornmeal or other coarse-ground gluten-free grains create a nice effect, too. Sometimes you'll have to nudge the loaves off with a spatula or dough scraper. Mostly, though, the choice of grain on the pizza peel is a matter of taste— Zoë's mom once used grits. If you're having trouble sliding loaves off a pizza peel prepared with grain, switch to parchment paper (see Equipment, page 38).

Dusting Flour: What Can I Use?

Throughout the book, whenever we call for dusting flour, we specify rice flour, because it's easy to work with in this situation. We don't recommend using strongly flavored flours like teff, sorghum, and garbanzo. And we don't like using starches (tapioca, cornstarch, arrowroot) for dusting, since they become gummy when they come into contact with wet dough. Coarse flours like cornmeal can get incorporated into the dough surface and alter its character. Brown or white rice flour will work, and so will Mixture #1 (see page 60).

Underbaking Problems

The crust is crispy when it emerges from the oven, but it softens as it comes to room temperature: The bread is underbaked. This is most often a problem with large breads, but it can happen with any loaf. Internal moisture, so high in gluten-free dough, doesn't dissipate in underbaked bread, so it redistributes to the crust as the bread cools. As you gain experience, you'll be able to judge just how brown the loaf must be to prevent this problem with any given loaf size. We use brownness and crust firmness as our measure of doneness.

The loaf has a soggy or gummy crumb (interior), even after it's cooled completely:

- Check your oven temperature with a thermometer, and be sure you're baking for the full time specified.
- Be sure that you're adequately preheating your stone and oven, and consider a longer preheat (see page 56).

Don't cut or eat loaves or flatbread when they're still warm. The proteins in the loaf continue to cook and set as they cool. Warm bread has a certain romance, so we know it's hard to wait. But waiting will improve the texture— loaf breads are at their peak of flavor and texture about two hours after they come out of the oven (or whenever they're completely cool). Hot or warm bread cuts poorly (the slices collapse) and dries out quickly, and all of these problems are exaggerated with high-moisture gluten-free dough. Use a sharp serrated bread knife to go right through the crisp crust and soft crumb.

- Make sure you are allowing the dough to rest for the full time period we've recommended.
- Be sure you're measuring your flour and liquids correctly, whether you opt for measuring cups or a scale.
- Your dough may benefit from being a little drier. For the next batch, increase the flour by ⅛ cup (or decrease the liquids a little) and check the result.
- If you're baking a large loaf (more than one pound), rest and bake it longer.

Top crust won't crisp and brown:

- **Consider using sugar in the dough:** Having a little sugar in the dough makes the top crust caramelize more easily, so our unsweetened dough recipes give you the option of adding some. This amount of sugar is not enough to change the flavor.
- **Use a hot baking stone** where called for, and preheat it for at least twenty to thirty minutes, in an oven whose temperature has been checked with a thermometer.
- **Bake with steam when called for:** Use one of the methods described on page 31.
- **Try the shelf switcheroo:** If you're a crisp-crust fanatic, here's the ultimate approach for baking the perfect crust. Place the stone on the bottom shelf and start the loaf there. Two-thirds of the way through baking, transfer the loaf from the stone directly to the top rack of the oven (leave the stone where it is). Top crusts brown best near the top of the oven, and bottom crusts brown best near the bottom. This approach works beautifully with free-form loaves, but also helps crisp the crust of hard-crusted loaf-pan breads: Just pop the bread out of

the pan before transferring to the top shelf—it makes a big difference. With this approach, you can permanently park your baking stone on the very lowest rack, where it will help even out the heat for everything you bake, not just bread. Then there'll be no need to shift around the stone or racks to accommodate your bread-baking habit.

Bottom crust is pale and soft:
This is commonly seen when the baking stone isn't fully preheated or when using parchment paper or silicone mats. If you want a crisper, browner bottom crust, pull the liner out from under the loaf about halfway through the baking. Or bake the loaf on cornmeal.

Frequently Asked Questions (FAQs) from Readers

"WHY DON'T MY GLUTEN-FREE LOAVES RISE MUCH DURING THE RESTING PERIOD AFTER SHAPING?"

Compared with wheat loaves, gluten-free loaves don't rise as much during the resting period after shaping, nor do they get quite as much "oven spring" (the sudden expansion of gasses inside the loaf that occurs on contact with hot oven air and baking stone). Gluten-free yeast breads get most of their rise and loft from the initial rise. **This is normal.**

"ARE GLUTEN-FREE BREADS DENSER THAN WHEAT BREADS?"

In general, yes. The gluten protein found in wheat creates a network that traps gas as it's produced by yeast, and this is what accounts for the vigorous rise that you get with wheat breads. In gluten-free yeast-baking, we're trying

Visit GFBreadIn5.com, where you'll find recipes, photos, videos, and instructional material.

to re-create that trapping effect with xanthan gum or ground psyllium husk (see page 22). It works, but don't expect as much rise and structure as you get with wheat. Because of that, it's even more important to allow the breads to cool completely—otherwise, they can seem gummy.

"MY LOAVES ARE TOO DENSE AND HEAVY— WHAT AM I DOING WRONG?"

If your bread is dense, doughy, or heavy, with poor hole structure . . .

1. If you're hand-mixing, consider switching to a stand mixer or food processor (see Equipment, page 42): Some people have trouble getting a smooth gluten-free mixture when they hand-mix. If your hand-mixed dough is lumpy, this can give you a dense loaf. If you're not happy with a hand-mixed batch, you can put it in a stand mixer, fitted with the paddle attachment, and let it run on high for 30 seconds to a minute. Let the dough rest for at least an hour before using as directed in the recipe.

2. Make sure that your dough is not too wet or too dry: Both extremes will result in a dense crumb. If you're measuring gluten-free flour by volume, make sure you are measuring by packing flour into the cup. And if you're getting inconsistent results, consider weighing the flour with a digital scale, rather than measuring it out with measuring cups (see "Tips and Techniques," page 46).

3. Be quick and gentle when shaping loaves: Many bakers, especially experienced ones, want to knead dough—but you can't do that with our soft gluten-free doughs. In the first place, it won't help anything, because there's no gluten to develop. Second, you'll knock the gas out of them and the result will be a dense crumb. When shaping our doughs, your goal is to preserve air bubbles as much as possible—these bubbles create the holes in the bread, which are so lovely and desirable. Shape your loaves gently, and don't try to stretch loaves into shape the way you do for wheat dough. Simply pat and shape with rice flour–dusted fingertips to smooth the surface (some recipes call for wet fingertips).

4. Try a longer rest after shaping, up to 90 minutes, especially if your kitchen is cool or you're making a large loaf: See Resting and Baking Times Are Approximate (page 49).

5. Check your oven temperature: See Equipment, page 35. If your oven's temperature is off, whether too warm or too cool, you won't get proper "oven spring" and the loaf will be dense, with a pale or burnt crust.

6. Try the "refrigerator rise" trick: By using the refrigerator, you can shape your dough and then have it rise in the refrigerator for 8 to 14 hours. **First thing in the morning,** pull off a piece of dough and shape it as you would normally. Place the dough on a sheet of parchment paper, loosely wrap with plastic or cover with an overturned bowl, and put it back in the refrigerator. **Right before dinner,** preheat your oven with a stone on a middle rack and take the loaf out of the refrigerator. You'll probably find that it hasn't risen much, but it will still get lovely oven spring. Because you don't handle the dough at all after the refrigerator rise, the bubbles in the dough should still be intact. A 20- to 30-minute rest while preheating is all you need. Then slash and bake as usual.

"HOW LONG SHOULD I PREHEAT MY BAKING STONE?"

Professionals sometimes suggest preheating the baking stone for an hour to absorb all the heat it possibly can, but we specify a shorter time in our recipes. Many of our readers expressed concern about wasted energy with a long preheat, not to mention the need for more advance planning. So we compromised. We know that some ovens will produce a crisper crust with a longer preheat, but we're pretty happy with the results we get at 20 to 30 minutes (even though many ovens equipped with a stone won't quite achieve target temperature that soon). If you find that the crust isn't as crisp as you like, or baking time is longer than expected, try increasing the preheating time to 45 or even 60 minutes. It's not essential but it can be useful, especially with a thicker stone.

Cast-iron or steel "stones" (see page 34) and ¼-inch-thick ceramic stones heat up faster than ½-inch-thick ceramic ones, so consider those if you're committed to the shortest possible preheat.

"WHAT IS 'LEAN' DOUGH?"

Lean doughs are those made without significant amounts of eggs, fat, dairy, or sweetener—basically, all the doughs in this book except those in Chapter 9. They bake well without burning or drying out at high temperatures.

Doughs "enriched" with lots of sweetener require a lower baking temperature (and a longer baking time), because they burn at high temperatures.

"WHAT'S THE BEST WAY TO STORE FRESHLY BAKED BREAD?"

We've found that the best way to keep bread fresh once it has been cut is to store it cut-side down on a flat, nonporous surface like a plate or a clean countertop. Don't store inside foil or plastic, which trap humidity and soften the crust by allowing it to absorb water. An exception is pita bread, which is supposed to have a soft crust and can be stored in a plastic bag or airtight container once cooled.

"CAN I FREEZE THE DOUGH?"

Our dough can be frozen at any point in its batch life, as long as the initial rise has been completed. It's best to carefully divide it into loaf-size portions, deflating as little as possible, then wrap it very well or seal in airtight containers. Defrost overnight in the fridge when ready to use, then shape, rest, and bake as usual. How long to freeze is partly a matter of taste—our dough loses some rising power when frozen, and some people find the breads dense if the dough's frozen for too long. Here are some basic guidelines for maximum freezing times:

- Lean dough (minimal eggs, butter, or oil): Four weeks
- Challah (see page 210): Three weeks
- Brioche (see page 216): Two weeks

"WHY DOES MY DOUGH HAVE A STRONG YEAST OR ALCOHOL SMELL?"

Some people detect a yeasty or alcohol aroma or flavor in breads made from stored dough, and that's no surprise—yeast multiplies in dough, creating alcohol and carbon dioxide gas as it ferments sugars and starches. The alcohol will boil off during baking, but our stored dough develops character from the by-products of yeast fermentation; most people appreciate the flavor and aroma of this mild sourdough. But others want less of that, so here are some things to try:

- Always vent the rising container as directed, especially in the first two days of storage (see pages 36–37). You can even poke a tiny hole in the lid to allow gas to escape.
- Store your dough for shorter periods than we specify, freezing the remainder. Or make smaller batches so they're used up more quickly.

5

THE FLOUR MIXTURES

O ur gluten-free experiments started in 2008, so we've known for years that our gluten-free breads tasted best when they were made with a **mixture** of gluten-free flours and xanthan gum or ground psyllium husk to provide structure. Otherwise, one flavor tended to predominate, or the texture was off. In our earlier books,

which included just a few gluten-free recipes, we didn't bother pre-mixing big bins of the flours, because we assumed that readers of those books were making gluten-free bread only occasionally and didn't need to keep the mixtures on hand. But once we started testing gluten-free recipes all the time, we found that pre-mixing is a huge time-saver. And as you've noticed, we place a premium on time-saving. There are only two mixtures you'll need to keep on hand to reap the benefits of pre-mixed gluten-free dough. Get some storage bins and flour and you're ready to start baking.

If you choose to use ground psyllium husk instead of xanthan gum, see sidebar, page 61.

Mixture #1: Gluten-Free All-Purpose Flour

This is our workhorse flour, a mixture of three gluten-free flours, plus a little xanthan gum (or ground psyllium) and potato starch. You can use either white or brown rice flour (see substitution opposite). Either way, you'll still benefit from whole grains because the sorghum flour typically available in the United States is whole grain. This flour blend yields a dough that makes beautiful free-form loaves, loaf-pan breads, and flat-breads. Add other flours, seeds, or flavorings to create great ethnic specialties like European Peasant Bread (page 96), Deli-Style "Rye" (page 109), Limpa (page 125), and others.

Makes about 4 1/4 pounds (2 kilograms) of flour mixture

Ingredient	Volume (U.S.), flour packed into measuring cups	Weight (U.S.)	Weight (Metric)
White rice flour*	6 cups	2 pounds, 4 ounces	1,020 grams
Sorghum flour*	3 1/4 cups	1 pound	455 grams
Tapioca flour or starch*	1 3/4 cups	8 ounces	225 grams
Potato starch	1 1/4 cups	8 ounces	225 grams
Xanthan gum or ground psyllium husk	1/4 cup	1.4 ounces	40 grams

*See flour substitutions (opposite)

The ingredients must be very well mixed, or the xanthan gum (or ground psyllium husk) will not be evenly distributed and your loaves will be inconsistent. Whisk and mix the ingredients in a 5- to 6-quart lidded

container (see pages 36–37). Finish by picking up the container and vigorously shaking until the flours are **completely** blended.

FLOUR SUBSTITUTIONS: If you are having a difficult time finding an ingredient, or prefer the taste of one over another, here are some tested substitutions you can use in our all-purpose flour blend.

Brown rice flour: Boost the whole grains by swapping brown rice flour for white rice flour; **you may need to add a couple more tablespoons of water to the dough as you mix.**
Sorghum flour can be replaced with **oat** or **amaranth flour.** Oat flour has a lighter color and more subtle flavor than sorghum or amaranth.

STARCH VARIATION: Arrowroot starch (the same as arrowroot flour) or **cornstarch** can be substituted for the tapioca starch.

Swapping ground psyllium husk for xanthan gum: If you choose not to use xanthan gum, you can swap ground psyllium husk, but some of the recipes call for an adjustment in its quantity. Enriched breads in Chapter 9 made with psyllium will look like cake batter until they are rested and chilled, at which time they may appear crumbly (but they bake up well). Don't store dough made with this substitution for longer than five days.

Visit GFBreadIn5.com, where you'll find recipes, photos, videos, and instructional material.

Mixture #2: 100% Whole-Grain Gluten-Free Flour

Keep a bin of this whole-grain flour around—it gives you terrific versatility, and it's lower in starch and higher in fiber than our all-purpose mix (page 60). If you're mixing by weight, you'll notice that this is pretty much the easiest recipe in the book, made from equal weights of four whole-grain flours, plus a little xanthan gum or ground psyllium husk.

Makes 4 pounds (1.85 kilograms) of flour mixture

Ingredient	Volume (U.S.), flour packed into measuring cups	Weight (U.S.)	Weight (Metric)
Brown rice flour*	3 cups *1 1/2*	1 pound	455 grams
Teff flour*	2 1/2 cups *1 1/4*	1 pound	455 grams
Sorghum flour*	3 1/4 cups *1 5/8*	1 pound	455 grams
Oat flour*	3 1/2 cups *1 3/4*	1 pound	455 grams
Xanthan gum or ground psyllium husk	1/4 cup *1/8* OR 1/2 cup *1/4*	1.4 ounces OR 2.8 ounces	40 grams OR 80 grams

*See flour substitutions (page 61)

The ingredients must be very well mixed, or the xanthan gum or ground psyllium husk will not be evenly distributed and your loaves will be inconsistent. Whisk and mix the ingredients in a 5- to 6-quart lidded container (see pages 36–37). Finish by picking up the container and vigorously shaking until the flours are **completely** blended.

6

THE MASTER RECIPE

We chose the artisan free-form loaf that the French call a *boule*—
pronounced "bool," meaning "ball"—as the basic model for all the
breads in this book (see color photo) and for our revolutionary
approach to bread baking: Take the needed amount of pre-mixed dough
from the refrigerator, shape it, leave it to rest, then pop it in the oven and
let it bake while you're preparing the rest of the meal.

The dough is made with nothing but gluten-free flour, yeast, salt, and
water, and it's easy to handle, shape, and bake successfully. Use it to make all
of the recipes in Chapter 6, and you'll be ready for the other techniques and
ingredients in the rest of the book. By mixing dough in bulk, and by storing
and using it as it's needed over time, you'll truly be able to make this bread
in five minutes a day (excluding resting and oven time). The standard version of the recipe was developed without eggs, since many gluten-free visitors
to our website told us that they were sensitive to eggs. **If eggs don't bother
you, you can also try a version of this recipe with eggs or egg whites, which
you'll find at the end of this recipe (see page 73).** Eggs create a slightly
lighter, airier loaf.

**You should become familiar with the following recipe before going
through the rest of the book.**

The Master Recipe: Boule (Gluten-Free Artisan Free-Form Loaf)

Makes four 1-pound loaves. The recipe is easily doubled or halved.

Ingredient	Volume (U.S.), flour packed into measuring cups	Weight (U.S.)	Weight (Metric)
Mixture #1: Gluten-Free All-Purpose (see page 60)	6$\frac{1}{2}$ cups	2 pounds, 3 ounces	990 grams
Granulated yeast	1 tablespoon	0.35 ounce	10 grams
Kosher salt[1]	1 to 1$\frac{1}{2}$ tablespoons	0.6 to 0.9 ounce	17 to 25 grams
Sugar (optional) (see page 52)	2 tablespoons	1 ounce	30 grams
Lukewarm water (100°F or below)	3$\frac{3}{4}$ cups	1 pound, 14 ounces	850 grams
Cornmeal or parchment paper, for the pizza peel			

[1] Can decrease (see page 25)

Mixing and Storing the Dough

1. **Measure the flour by packing it tightly into dry-ingredient measuring cups, or weigh the ingredients (see photographs, page 61).** Whisk together the flour, yeast, salt, and sugar (if using) in a 5- to 6-quart bowl, or a lidded (not airtight) food container.

2. **Warm the water slightly.** It should feel just a little warmer than body temperature, about 100°F. Warm water allows the dough to rise to the right point for storage in about 2 hours.

3. **Add the water and mix with a spoon or a heavy-duty stand mixer fitted with the paddle attachment** (see page 42). If using the machine, mix slowly at first to prevent sloshing, and then increase the speed to medium-high. Continue to mix until very smooth, about

Visit GFBreadIn5.com, where you'll find recipes, photos, videos, and instructional material.

1 minute. **Kneading is unnecessary.** If you're hand-mixing, it will take longer to reach a smooth consistency. See the sidebar on page 68 for a shortcut to a superfast first loaf.

4. **Allow to rise.** Cover with a lid that fits well to the container but can be cracked open so it's not completely airtight—most plastic lids fit the bill, but so does a lid on a soup pot. If you're using an ordinary mixing bowl, cover it loosely with plastic wrap. Most stand mixer bowls can be fitted with a matching plastic lid that can be cracked open for venting, or are non-sealing in the first place. Towels don't work—they stick to wet dough. Lidded (or even vented) plastic buckets are readily available (see pages 36–37).

Other tools to use for the initial mix: If you're mixing by hand, a **Danish dough whisk** is an effective alternative to a wooden spoon. It's much stouter than a flimsy egg-beating whisk and does a nice job incorporating wet and dry ingredients. **Food processors** also work—just replace the standard blade with the dough attachment that comes with most machines. Make sure the machine is rated to handle dough—the motor must be heavy duty. You'll also need the largest size made to mix a full batch—one with a 14-cup bowl. Make a half batch if your processor has a smaller bowl.

Visit GFBreadIn5.com, where you'll find recipes, photos, videos, and instructional material.

Allow the mixture to rise at room temperature, about 2 hours, depending on the room's temperature and the initial water temperature—then refrigerate it and use over the next 10 days. If your container isn't vented, allow gasses to escape by leaving it open a crack for the first couple of days in the fridge—after that you can usually close it. You can use a portion of the dough any time after the 2-hour rise. **Relax! You don't need to monitor doubling or tripling of volume as in traditional recipes.** Fully refrigerated wet dough is less sticky and is easier to work with than dough at room temperature, so the first time you try our method, it's best to refrigerate the dough overnight (or for at least 3 hours) before shaping a loaf. Whatever you do, **do not punch down this dough.** With our method, you're trying to retain as much gas in the dough as possible, and punching it down knocks gas out and will make your loaves denser.

◌◌

No rest, no rise, just bake: If you are in a big rush you can forgo the initial rise altogether. Just mix the dough with warm water, pull off a 1-pound piece, shape it on a piece of parchment paper, and put it in a cold oven. Set the oven temperature to 400°F and bake for 75 minutes. This only works with freshly made dough; once it is refrigerated, follow the normal directions. Although this is superfast, you will end up with a denser loaf and the flavor won't be as complex. But, sometimes we're just in a hurry.

On Baking Day

5. **Shape the loaf.** Pull off a 1-pound (grapefruit-size) piece, then place it on a pizza peel prepared with cornmeal (use plenty) or parchment paper. (If you'd like to avoid sliding the loaf off a pizza peel, you can also bake it on a heavy-gauge baking sheet prepared with butter, oil, parchment paper, or a silicone mat.) This dough does not stretch—and can't be stretched, because there is no gluten in it—just gently press and pat it into shape, and use wet fingers to smooth the surface. Allow to rest for 60 minutes (see sidebar, page 70), loosely covered with plastic wrap or a roomy overturned bowl. The dough may not seem to rise much, which is normal for this dough. **For a video of the shaping step, visit GFBreadIn5.com.**

6. **Preheat a baking stone near the middle of the oven to 450°F,** which takes 20 to 30 minutes (you may consider a longer preheat; see page 34). Place an empty metal broiler tray for holding water on

Visit GFBreadIn5.com, where you'll find recipes, photos, videos, and instructional material.

Shortening the resting time: Rest for half as long if you're using fresh, unrefrigerated dough.

Lengthening the resting time: If you're making a larger loaf, you'll get better results with a 90-minute resting time. Try this with the 1-pound loaf if you're finding that the 60-minute rest gives you a denser result than you'd like.

any shelf that won't interfere with rising bread. **Never use a glass pan to catch water for steam—it's likely to shatter.**

7. **Dust and slash:** Dust the top of the loaf liberally with flour. Slash a $\frac{1}{2}$-inch-deep cross, scallop, or tic-tac-toe into the top, using a wet serrated bread knife held perpendicular to the bread (see photos). You may need to wipe off the blade after each slash. Leave the flour in place for baking; tap some of it off before eating.

8. **Baking with steam—slide the loaf onto the preheated stone.** Place the tip of the peel a few inches beyond where you want the bread to land. Give the peel a few quick forward-and-back jiggles, and pull it sharply out from under the loaf. Quickly but carefully pour about 1 cup of hot water from the tap into the metal broiler tray and close the oven door to trap the steam (see page 31 for steam alternatives). **If you used parchment paper instead of cornmeal, pull it out from under the loaf after about 20 minutes** for a crisper bottom crust. Bake for about **45 minutes total,** or until the crust is richly browned and firm to the touch (larger or smaller loaves will require adjustments in baking time). When you remove the loaf from the oven, a perfectly baked loaf will audibly crackle, or "sing," when initially exposed to room-temperature air. Allow to cool completely (up to 2 hours), preferably on a wire cooling rack, for best flavor, texture, and slicing. **Never eat gluten-free loaf breads warm, or they may seem underdone on the inside—they need plenty of time to set completely.**

⁀

Instant-read thermometers: We're not in love with internal-temperature food thermometers, usually sold as "instant-read" thermometers (as opposed to oven thermometers, which we love—see page 35). They have a pointed probe that you stick into the bread to see if it has reached a target temperature. We find that the inexpensive ones (under $20) aren't all that "instant," which means that you're never sure how long to wait before the readout stabilizes. The truly instant (and accurate) digital units are much more expensive (but can still give misleading results if your probe's not well centered in the loaf). If you have confidence in your thermometer and your technique, here are some guidelines for fully baked bread:

- Lean dough with minimal eggs or sweeteners (all the doughs in the book except for those in Chapter 9): 205°F (96°C to 99°C)

- Egg-enriched dough, such as Challah and Brioche (Chapter 9): 180°F to 185°F (82°C to 85°C)

9. **Store the remaining dough in the refrigerator in your lidded or loosely plastic-wrapped container and use it over the next 10 days.** By storing the dough in the same container that you mixed in, you'll avoid some cleanup. Pull off dough and shape more loaves as you need them. This dough can be also be frozen in 1-pound portions, well wrapped or in an airtight container for up to 4 weeks and defrosted overnight in the refrigerator before use.

Lazy sourdough shortcut: When your dough bucket is finally empty, or nearly so, don't wash it. Immediately remix another batch in the same container. In addition to saving the cleanup step, the aged dough stuck to the sides of the container will give your new batch a head start on sourdough flavor. Just scrape it down and it will hydrate and incorporate into the new dough. **Don't do this with egg- or dairy-enriched dough**—with those, the container should be washed after each use.

You can take this even further by adding a more sizable amount of old dough from your last batch. You can use up to 2 cups; just mix it in with the water for your new batch and let it stand until it becomes soupy before you start mixing. Professionals call this *pâte fermentée* (pot fair-mon-táy), which means nothing more than "fermented dough."

VARIATION: FREE-FORM LOAF WITH EGGS OR EGG WHITES FOR EXTRA RISE

Some of our testers who wanted to use eggs preferred the lighter texture and airier crumb you get when you add eggs to gluten-free doughs.

Follow the directions for the Master Recipe, but when you're ready to measure the water, place 4 large eggs or egg whites into the bottom of a measuring cup, then add water to bring the total volume to 3¾ cups of liquid. If you're measuring by weight, zero (tare) your weighing container, then put 4 eggs into it. Add water to bring the total weight to 1 pound, 14 ounces/850 grams. Egg doughs should be frozen after 5 days of refrigeration in 1-pound portions. Bake this egg-enriched dough at 450°F for 45 minutes.

VARIATION: SEEDED BREADS

Seeds give added flavor and character to gluten-free breads. Omit the flour-dusting step, and paint with water and then sprinkle with seeds before baking (sesame, flaxseed, caraway, sunflower, poppy, anise, or a mixture of any of these).

You can also put the seeds right in the dough mixture—try ¼ cup of seeds per batch.

VARIATION: HERB BREAD

Adding zesty or distinctive flavors like herbs is the easiest variation of all. If you love an herb bread from your wheat-eating days, try it gluten-free. Herb-scented breads are great favorites for appetizers and snacks.

Follow the directions for mixing the Master Recipe and add 1 teaspoon dried thyme leaves (or 2 teaspoons fresh) and ½ teaspoon dried rosemary leaves (or 1 teaspoon fresh) to the water mixture. You can also use herbs with the other recipes in this chapter.

Baguette

In France, this thin and crusty loaf is served at every meal—it's the symbol of an entire cuisine (see color photo). It turns out that you can make a gorgeous and delicious gluten-free baguette. Aside from the shaping, one important technique that differentiates the baguette from the boule in this chapter is that the baguette is *not* heavily dusted with flour, at least not traditionally. So, to keep the knife from sticking, wet the top crust just before slashing.

Makes 1 baguette

½ pound (orange-size portion) Master Recipe dough (page 64)
1 egg white plus 1 tablespoon water, or plain water, for brushing the loaf
Parchment paper or a silicone mat, for the pizza peel or baking sheet

1. Dust the surface of the dough and pull off a ½-pound (orange-size) piece and place it on a pizza peel prepared with parchment paper or a baking sheet prepared with a silicone mat. Shape it

Visit GFBreadIn5.com, where you'll find recipes, photos, videos, and instructional material.

into a skinny cylinder with pointed ends. This dough does not stretch, so just press, squeeze, and pat into a baguette using flour-dusted hands. Once the baguette is shaped, smooth the surface with wet fingers. Cover loosely with plastic wrap and allow to rest and rise for 40 minutes (see sidebar in Master Recipe step 5, page 70).

2. **Preheat a baking stone near the middle of the oven to 450°F (20 to 30 minutes),** with an empty metal broiler tray on any shelf that won't interfere with rising bread.

3. Brush the top with egg white wash or water and then slash with diagonal cuts, about ½ inch deep, with a wet serrated bread knife.

4. Slide the loaf onto the hot stone. Pour 1 cup of hot tap water into the broiler tray, and quickly close the oven door (see page 31 for steam alternatives). Bake for **about 35 minutes,** or until richly browned and firm. Smaller or larger loaves will require adjustments in resting and baking time.

5. Allow to cool on a rack before eating.

Bâtard (báh-tar)

The *bâtard*, a short and wide French loaf with pointed ends, is more suitable to use for sandwiches than a baguette. It's the same shape used for traditional rye-style loaves. If you like, you can make the bâtard almost as wide as a sandwich loaf, but traditionally it is about three inches across at its widest point. Like a baguette, the bâtard is tapered to a point at each end—it's sometimes described as "torpedo-shaped."

Makes 1 bâtard

1 pound (grapefruit-size portion) Master Recipe dough (page 64)
1 egg white plus 1 tablespoon water or plain water, for brushing the loaf
Cornmeal or parchment paper, for the pizza peel

1. Follow steps 1 and 2 for the baguette on page 75, but shape the loaf to a diameter of about 3 inches.

2. Follow steps 3 through 5 for the baguette, but increase the resting time to 60 minutes and the baking time to 40 minutes (or until deeply brown).

VARIATION: ITALIAN BREAD
In the United States, a torpedo-shaped loaf topped with sesame seeds is usually referred to as Italian bread. No wonder—in Italy, sesame seeds find their way onto all sorts of traditional loaves. If you want to make this gluten-free loaf Italian-style, brush it with egg white wash or water, then sprinkle with sesame seeds just before baking.

Ciabatta (cha-báh-tah)

The word *ciabatta* is Italian for "slipper," and refers to the shape of the bread, which is halfway between a flatbread and a loaf. It's shaped as an elongated flattened oval or rectangle—perhaps you have slippers shaped like this? Ciabattas make fantastic sandwiches when split and filled—allow to cool first.

Makes 1 ciabatta

1 pound (grapefruit-size portion) Master Recipe dough (page 64)
Parchment paper, for the pizza peel

1. Pull off a 1-pound (grapefruit-size) piece of dough and place it on a pizza peel prepared with parchment. Using wet fingers, quickly shape and then flatten into an elongated oval about ¾ inch thick. Dust the top with rice flour and cover loosely with plastic wrap or an overturned bowl and allow to rest for 30 minutes.

2. **Preheat a baking stone near the middle of the oven to 450°F (20 to 30 minutes),** with an empty metal broiler tray on any shelf that won't interfere with rising bread.

3. Remove the plastic wrap and dust with more flour if most of it has come off or been absorbed.

4. Slide the loaf onto the hot stone, pour 1 cup of hot tap water into the broiler tray, and quickly close the oven door (see page 31 for steam alternatives). Bake for **about 35 minutes,** or until richly

browned and firm. If you notice puffing during baking, poke the air bubbles with a long-handled fork. Smaller or larger loaves will require adjustments in resting and baking time.

5. Allow to cool on a rack before eating.

Couronne (cor-ówn)

This ring, or crown-shaped, French loaf is a specialty of Lyon. The *couronne* is quite simple to shape and is a beautiful, crustier alternative to the classic boule (see color photo).

Makes 1 couronne

1 pound (grapefruit-size portion) Master Recipe dough (page 64)
Parchment paper, for the pizza peel

1. Dust the top of the dough with flour, pull off a 1-pound (grapefruit-size) piece, and place it on a pizza peel prepared with parchment paper. Quickly shape it into a ball and smooth the surface by gently pressing with flour-dusted fingers.

2. Poke your thumbs through the center of the ball and gently stretch the hole so that it is about three times as wide as the wall of the ring, adding more flour to prevent the dough from sticking to your hands. Once the couronne is shaped, smooth the surface with wet fingers.

3. Cover loosely with plastic wrap or an overturned bowl and allow to rest for 40 minutes (see sidebar in Master Recipe step 5, page 70).

4. **Preheat a baking stone near the middle of the oven to 450°F (20 to 30 minutes),** with an empty metal broiler tray on any shelf that won't interfere with rising bread.

5. Dust with rice flour and slash radially, like spokes in a wheel, about ½ inch deep (see color photo).

6. Slide the loaf onto the hot stone. Pour 1 cup of hot tap water into the broiler tray, and quickly close the oven door (see page 31 for steam alternatives). Bake for **about 35 minutes,** or until richly browned and firm. Smaller or larger loaves will require adjustments in resting and baking time.

7. Allow to cool on a rack before eating.

Pain d'Epí (pan deh-peé)

We had a good laugh over this one, because our early drafts of this book translated the French expression *pain d'epi* as "bread of the wheat stalk"—a complete no-no in a no-wheat book. But really, *pain d'epi* means "bread of the ear," as in "ear of corn" or "ear of wheat" (you don't hear that last one much in English). We think it's lovely that the French have a special word for this, *epi* (as opposed to *oreille*, which is a person's ear). Why are grain stalks said to have ears? Well, if you look at them, most grains, including gluten-free ones, stick out at an angle to either side of the stalk (and yes, some of us have ears like this). Since the word *epi* isn't particular to wheat, we've kept it, with its more accurate translation. Fancifully shaped like a stalk of grain, the pain d'epi is a simple yet impressive bread to present to guests (see color photo).

Makes 1 pain d'epi

½ pound (orange-size portion) Master Recipe dough (page 64)
Parchment paper or a silicone mat, for the pizza peel or baking sheet

1. Dust the surface of the dough and pull off a ½-pound (orange-size) piece and place it on a pizza peel prepared with parchment paper or a baking sheet prepared with a silicone mat. Shape it into a skinny cylinder with pointed ends. This dough does not stretch, so just press, squeeze, and pat it into a baguette using flour-dusted hands. Once the baguette is shaped, smooth the surface with wet fingers. Cover loosely with plastic wrap and allow to rest for 40 minutes (see sidebar in Master Recipe step 5, page 70).

2. Dust the loaf lightly with rice flour. Using kitchen shears and starting at one end of the loaf, cut into the dough at a very shallow angle. If you cut too vertically, the "grains" won't be as pointy. Cut with a single snip to within ¼ inch of the work surface, but be careful not to cut all the way through the loaf or you'll have separate rolls (see photos above).

3. As you cut, lay each piece over to one side. Continue to cut in this fashion until you've reached the end of the stalk, wiping the blades of the shears clean after each cut (see photos above).

4. **Preheat a baking stone near the middle of the oven to 450°F (20 to 30 minutes),** with an empty metal broiler tray on any shelf that won't interfere with rising bread.

5. Slide the loaf onto the hot stone. Pour 1 cup of hot tap water into the broiler tray and quickly close the oven door (see page 31 for

steam alternatives). Bake for **about 30 minutes,** or until richly browned and firm. Smaller or larger loaves will require adjustments in resting and baking time.

6. Allow to cool on a rack before eating.

Crusty White Sandwich Loaf

This is a hearty, crusty bread that will hold up to the beefiest sandwich fillings. Removing the loaf from the pan for the last ten minutes of baking will allow the sides of the loaf to color and crisp. Nonstick pans release more easily, but you can use a traditional loaf pan if it's heavy gauge and you grease it well; otherwise, the loaf is likely to stick. You can use this method with any of our doughs.

Makes 1 loaf

2 pounds (cantaloupe-size portion) Master Recipe dough (page 64)
Water, for brushing the loaf
Oil or butter, for greasing the pan

1. Grease an 8½ × 4½-inch nonstick loaf pan (grease heavily if you're not using a nonstick pan).

2. Using wet hands, pull off a 2-pound (cantaloupe-size) piece of dough and drop it into the prepared pan. Smooth the top of the loaf with water.

3. Cover loosely with plastic wrap or an over-turned bowl and allow to rest for 90 minutes (see sidebar in Master Recipe step 5, page 70).

4. **Preheat a baking stone near the middle of the oven to 425°F (20 to 30 minutes),** with an empty metal broiler tray on any shelf that won't interfere with rising bread. The stone isn't required for loaf-pan breads and if you omit it, the preheat can be as short as 5 minutes.

5. Brush the top with water, and then slash, about ½ inch deep, with a wet serrated bread knife.

6. Put the pan in the oven on a middle shelf, pour 1 cup of hot tap water into the broiler tray, and quickly close the oven door

> ∽
>
> **It's not absolutely necessary to slash breads baked in a pan:** A loaf pan or a small cast-iron pot will prevent shape problems. The top crust may crack open randomly but it won't be mis-shapen.

(see page 31 for steam alternatives). Bake for **55 to 60 minutes,** or until richly browned and firm. Smaller or larger loaves will require adjustments in resting and baking time.

7. Remove the loaf from the pan; if the loaf sticks, wait 10 minutes and it will steam itself out of the pan.

8. Allow to cool completely on a rack before slicing; otherwise, you won't get well-cut slices.

Crock Pot Bread (Fast Bread in a Slow Cooker)

Everyone loves crock pots, bubbling away with Swedish meatballs, no-peek chicken, or chili. Over the years we've had requests for a method for baking our dough in one. **Bread in a crock pot? We had our doubts, lots of them.** We didn't think a slow cooker could get hot enough; thought it would take too long; didn't think it would bake through or have a nice crust. So we resisted trying it, convinced it would fail. **Oh, how wrong we were** (see back cover photo). The crock pot does indeed get hot enough, and it takes less time than using your oven because the rising time is included in the baking. Straight out of the pot, the crust is soft and quite pale, but just a few minutes under the broiler and you have a gorgeous loaf. And in summertime, no need to heat up the oven to get great bread. You could even amaze your friends at work by baking a loaf under your desk.

Makes 1 loaf

1 pound (grapefruit-size portion) Master Recipe dough (page 64)
Parchment paper, for shaping and baking

1. Pull off a 1-pound (grapefruit-size) piece of dough. Place it on a piece of parchment paper dusted with rice flour and quickly shape into a ball, gently smoothing with wet fingers.

2. Lower the dough, parchment paper and all, into a crock pot or other slow cooker. Be sure to follow the manufacturer's instructions for proper use.

3. Turn the temperature to high and put on the cover.

4. Bake for about **1 hour and 15 minutes** (the time will depend on your slow cooker; you may need to increase or decrease the time). Keep an eye on the loaf starting at 45 minutes to make sure it is not overbrowning on the bottom or not browning at all. You may need to adjust the time according to your appliance. **To check for doneness,** it should feel firm when you gently poke the top of the loaf.

5. The bottom crust should be nice and crisp, but the top of the loaf will be quite soft. Some folks desire a softer crust, so they'll love this loaf.

6. For a darker, crisper crust, peel off the parchment paper and, with the rack positioned in the middle of the oven, place the bread under the broiler for 5 minutes, or until it is the color you like.

Check with your crock pot's manufacturer before trying this recipe: Some models' instructions specify that the pot has to be at least partially filled with a liquid to avoid safety or durability problems—which wouldn't work here! And never bake bread in an unattended crock pot.

7. Allow to cool on a rack before eating.

Soft Dinner Rolls, Brötchen, and Baguette Buns

Rolls are fast and easy to make. Because of their size, the dough warms up quickly, so they need very little resting time before they go into the oven. You can make any of the following recipes with the Master Recipe, or try these easy shapes with other lean doughs, or even the enriched Challah (page 210) or Brioche (page 216) doughs. **Be sure to decrease the oven temperature to 350°F and increase the baking time about 25 percent when using egg-enriched dough.**

Makes five 3-ounce rolls

1 pound (grapefruit-size portion) Master Recipe dough (page 64), Egg-White Enriched dough (see page 73), or Peasant doughs (pages 95–169)
For brötchen: Egg white wash (1 egg white mixed with 1 teaspoon water), for glazing
Melted unsalted butter or oil, for brushing the tops
Silicone mat or parchment paper, for the baking sheet

Soft dinner rolls

1. **Preheat a baking stone near the middle of the oven to 350°F (20 to 30 minutes).**

2. Dust the surface of the dough with rice flour, pull off five 3-ounce (small peach–size) pieces of Brioche or Challah dough, and quickly shape into balls. Allow to rest, 2 inches apart, on a baking sheet lined with parchment paper or a silicone mat for 30 minutes.

∽

To make soft pull-apart rolls (see color photo): Pull out a 1¹/₂-pound (small cantaloupe–size) piece of Challah (page 210), Brioche (page 216), or Buttermilk Bread dough (page 247), then divide the dough into 8 pieces and quickly shape into balls. Place the balls in a greased 8 × 8-inch baking dish; they should be touching. Rest for 40 minutes. Preheat the oven to 350°F. Brush the tops of the rolls with melted butter or oil before they go into the oven and again when they come out. Bake for **30 to 35 minutes,** or until golden brown. Allow to cool on a rack before serving.

3. Cut a cross into the top of each roll using kitchen shears, keeping the shears perpendicular to the work surface when you cut.

4. Brush the tops with melted butter or oil, and place the baking sheet in the oven. Bake for **about 25 minutes,** or until richly browned.

5. For the softest result, brush with more butter or oil.

6. Allow to cool on a rack before serving.

Brötchen (bro-chin)

On our website, people asked for German-style rolls, so we've included the most common: *brötchen* (German for "little bread"—see color photo). They're traditionally made from dough enriched with egg whites, and then brushed with more egg white before baking at high temperature with steam. The egg white creates a wonderful crust and crumb—see page 73 in the Master Recipe for an easy variation that turns the Master Recipe into brötchen dough for these superb German-style rolls (though it can be used for other purposes as well).

1. **Preheat the oven to 450°F,** with an empty metal broiler tray on any shelf that won't interfere with rising brötchen.

2. Dust the dough with rice flour and pull off 3-ounce (small peach–size) pieces of egg white–enriched dough (see Master Recipe variation, page 73) and quickly shape into balls, then squeeze to form oval shapes. Allow to rest, 2 inches apart, on a baking sheet prepared with oil, butter, parchment paper, or a silicone mat for 30 minutes.

3. Brush the tops with egg white wash and cut a single lengthwise slash into the top of each roll using a serrated knife.

4. Place the baking sheet in the oven, pour 1 cup of hot tap water into the broiler tray, and quickly close the oven door (see page 31 for steam alternatives). Bake the rolls for **about 25 minutes,** or until richly browned.

5. Allow to cool on a rack before serving.

Baguette Buns (see color photo)

1. **Preheat a baking stone near the middle of the oven to 450°F (20 to 30 minutes),** with an empty metal broiler tray on any other shelf.

2. Form a ½-pound baguette (see page 75) on a work surface; this will make about 6 buns. Dust the baguette with rice flour, and then use a dough scraper or a knife to make angled parallel cuts about 2 inches apart along the length of the baguette to form rolls. Allow them to rest, 2 inches apart, directly on a baking sheet prepared with oil, butter, parchment paper, or a silicone mat, for 20 to 25 minutes.

3. Place the baking sheet in the oven, pour 1 cup of hot tap water into the broiler tray, and quickly close the oven door. Bake the rolls for **about 25 minutes,** or until richly browned.

4. Allow to cool on a rack before serving.

7

PEASANT LOAVES

The term "peasant bread" has come to mean the rougher, more rustic loaf that originated in the European countryside during the Middle Ages. These are breads made with whole-grain ingredients that, once upon a time, fell out of fashion with sophisticated European urbanites. How times have changed; since the 1980s, rustic breads have signaled sophistication just as surely as a perfect French baguette. Thank goodness we've come to realize the wonderful and complex flavors to be had by adding whole grains to our bread.

Rye and other gluten-containing grains were at the heart of these loaves, so our job was to re-create their tangy, slightly nutty fragrance and flavor with something else—so we did it with teff, brown rice, sorghum, flax, corn, almond, coconut, buckwheat, quinoa, and oats. This is your chance to put more whole grains into your gluten-free baking, including a 100% Whole-Grain Loaf (see page 102).

European Peasant Bread (Light Whole Grain)

∽

Super-Six nutrition-boosters (see page 11): Substitute ¹/₂ cup amaranth, buckwheat, millet, or quinoa flour for the same amount of Mixture #2. **Or try a protein boost** with ¹/₂ cup of legume flours: garbanzo, soy, peanut, or pea in place of the same amount of Mixture #2.

The round, whole-grain, country-style loaves of rural France (*pain de campagne*) and Italy (*pane rustica*) were once viewed as too rustic for stylish European tables—white flour was once an almost-unattainable luxury. Today people from all walks of life enjoy the hearty, moist, and chewy crumb that defines this peasant bread—the key is more whole grains. For even more whole grains, consider using the brown rice flour substitution in Mixture #1 (page 61).

Makes four loaves, slightly more than 1 pound each. The recipe is easily doubled or halved.

Ingredient	Volume (U.S.), flour packed into measuring cups	Weight (U.S.)	Weight (Metric)
Mixture #1: Gluten-Free All-Purpose Flour (see page 60)	6 cups	2 pounds	910 grams
Mixture #2: 100% Whole-Grain Gluten-Free Flour (see page 62)	1 cup	5¹/₂ ounces	155 grams

(continued)

Ingredient	Volume (U.S.), flour packed into measuring cups	Weight (U.S.)	Weight (Metric)
Granulated yeast	1 tablespoon	0.35 ounce	10 grams
Kosher salt[1]	1 to 1½ tablespoons	0.6 to 0.9 ounce	17 to 25 grams
Sugar (optional)	2 tablespoons	1 ounce	30 grams
Lukewarm water (100°F or below)	4¼ cups	2 pounds, 2 ounces	965 grams
Cornmeal or parchment paper, for the pizza peel			

[1]Can decrease (see pages 25)

1. **Mixing and storing the dough:** Whisk together the flours, yeast, salt, and sugar (if using) in a 5- to 6-quart bowl, or any lidded (not airtight) food container.

2. Add the water and mix with a spoon or heavy-duty stand mixer fitted with the paddle attachment (see page 42).

3. Cover (not airtight), and allow to rest at room temperature until the dough rises, approximately 2 hours.

4. The dough can be used immediately after the initial rise, though it is easier to handle when cold. Refrigerate it in a lidded (not airtight) container and use over the next 10 days. Or freeze for up to 4 weeks in 1-pound portions and thaw in the refrigerator overnight before use.

5. **On baking day:** Pull off a 1-pound (grapefruit-size) piece of dough. Place it on a pizza peel prepared with cornmeal (use plenty) or

parchment paper. Quickly shape it into a ball and smooth the surface with wet fingers. Cover loosely with plastic wrap or an overturned bowl and allow to rest for 60 minutes (see sidebar in Master Recipe, page 70).

6. **Preheat a baking stone near the middle of the oven to 450°F (20 to 30 minutes),** with an empty metal broiler tray on any shelf that won't interfere with rising bread.

7. Dust the top with rice flour and slash, about ½ inch deep, with a wet serrated bread knife (see photos page 70).

8. Slide the loaf onto the hot stone. Pour 1 cup of hot tap water into the broiler tray, and quickly close the oven door (see page 31 for steam alternatives). Bake for **about 45 minutes,** or until richly browned and firm. Smaller or larger loaves will require adjustments in resting and baking time.

9. Allow to cool on a rack before eating.

Whole-Grain Gluten-Free Loaf (No Eggs, 50% Whole Grains)

Many gluten-free recipes use eggs to give the dough a little extra rising power, and that becomes more important when you start increasing the whole grain in a recipe. But we found that we could bake excellent, egg-free *and* gluten-free recipes that included up to about 50 percent whole grains. There are two advantages to no-egg dough. First, some of our gluten-free readers told us that they were also avoiding eggs. Second, egg-enriched dough can only be stored in the refrigerator for a maximum of five days, and we wanted to be able to make an everyday bread, with lots of whole grains, that could store for ten days—the longer you can store, the more convenient the recipe. So here's a terrific whole-grain loaf, without any eggs, that stores for ten days in the refrigerator. If you want 100 percent whole-grain loaves, you'll need some eggs (see 100% Whole-Grain Loaf, page 102).

Ingredient	Volume (U.S.), flour packed into measuring cups	Weight (U.S.)	Weight (Metric)
Mixture #1: Gluten-Free All-Purpose Flour (see page 60)	3½ cups	1 pound, 3 ounces	540 grams
Mixture #2: 100% Whole-Grain Gluten-Free Flour (see page 62)	3½ cups	1 pound, 3 ounces	540 grams
Granulated yeast	1 tablespoon	0.35 ounce	10 grams

(continued)

Visit GFBreadIn5.com, where you'll find recipes, photos, videos, and instructional material.

Ingredient	Volume (U.S.), flour packed into measuring cups	Weight (U.S.)	Weight (Metric)
Kosher salt[1]	1 to 1½ tablespoons	0.6 to 0.9 ounce	17 to 25 grams
Sugar (optional)	2 tablespoons	1 ounce	30 grams
Lukewarm water (100°F or below)	4¾ cups	2 pounds, 6 ounces	1,080 grams
Cornmeal or parchment paper, for the pizza peel			

[1]Can decrease (see page 25)

Makes five loaves, slightly more than 1 pound each. The recipe is easily doubled or halved.

1. **Mixing and storing the dough:** Whisk together the flours, yeast, salt, and sugar (if using) in a 5- to 6-quart bowl, or a lidded (not airtight) food container.

2. Add the water and mix with a spoon or a heavy-duty stand mixer fitted with the paddle attachment (see page 42).

3. Cover (not airtight), and allow to rest at room temperature until the dough rises, approximately 2 hours.

4. The dough can be used immediately after the initial rise, though it is easier to handle when cold. Refrigerate it in a lidded (not airtight) container and use over the next 10 days. Or freeze for up to 4 weeks in 1-pound portions and thaw in the refrigerator overnight before use.

5. **On baking day:** Pull off a 1-pound (grapefruit-size) piece of dough. Place it on a pizza peel prepared with cornmeal (use plenty) or parchment paper. Quickly shape it into a ball and smooth the surface with wet fingers. Cover loosely with plastic wrap or an overturned bowl and allow to rest for 60 minutes (see sidebar in Master Recipe, page 70).

6. **Preheat a baking stone near the middle of the oven to 450°F (20 to 30 minutes),** with an empty metal broiler tray on any shelf that won't interfere with rising bread.

7. Dust the top with rice flour and slash, about ½ inch deep, with a wet serrated bread knife (see photos page 70).

8. Slide the loaf onto the hot stone. Pour 1 cup of hot tap water into the broiler tray, and quickly close the oven door (see page 31 for steam alternatives). Bake for **about 45 minutes,** or until richly browned and firm. Smaller or larger loaves will require adjustments in resting and baking time.

9. Allow to cool on a rack before eating.

100% Whole-Grain Loaf

For this 100 percent whole-grain loaf, we call for eggs—because eggs lighten whole-grain bread, and we found that this was especially important with our stored gluten-free loaves. Crunchy whole millet seeds add delightful earthy flavor. The touch of molasses adds color and provides rich, deep flavor, and its natural sugars tenderize the loaf. You can swap it for other sweeteners, but they won't lend as much color. The buckwheat variation (page 105) is one of our favorite loaves in the book.

On our website, people asked us whether they could use wicker rising baskets (*banneton* in French, or *brotform* in German) to contain the dough and prevent it from spreading sideways during rising. We were a bit skeptical, fearing that dough this wet might stick to the wicker. But so long as you coat it heavily with rice flour, it's not a problem. This is a gorgeous and visually dramatic way to bake any of our breads. The dough rises in contact with the wicker rings, and as a result it's ringed with scorched flour when it's baked (see color photo). The smaller *bannetons* are a bit difficult to find, but it's worth seeking out a 6½-inch one. **If you don't have a banneton, this dough bakes up beautifully as a free-form bread (follow instructions for Whole-Grain Gluten-Free Loaf on page 99).**

Makes five loaves, about 1 pound each. The recipe is easily doubled or halved.

Ingredient	Volume (U.S.), flour packed into measuring cups	Weight (U.S.)	Weight (Metric)
Mixture #2: 100% Whole-Grain Gluten-Free Flour (see page 62)	5¾ cups	2 pounds	910 grams
Millet flour	½ cup	3 ounces	85 grams
Millet (whole, not ground)	½ cup	3½ ounces	100 grams
Xanthan gum[1]	2 teaspoons	—	—
Granulated yeast	1 tablespoon	0.35 ounce	10 grams
Kosher salt[2]	1 to 1½ tablespoons	0.6 to 0.9 ounce	17 to 25 grams
Lukewarm water (100°F or below)	4 cups	2 pounds	910 grams
Molasses, honey, or agave syrup	¼ cup	2½ ounces	70 grams
Large eggs	4	8 ounces	225 grams
Cornmeal or parchment paper, for the pizza peel			

[1]If you used psyllium instead of xanthan gum in Mixture #2, do not use xanthan gum here.
[2]Can decrease (see page 25)

1. **Mixing and storing the dough:** Whisk together the flours, grains, yeast and salt in a 5- to 6-quart bowl, or a lidded (not airtight) food container.

2. Add the water, sweetener, and eggs, and mix with a spoon or a heavy-duty stand mixer fitted with the paddle attachment (see page 42).

3. Cover (not airtight), and allow to rest at room temperature until the dough rises, approximately 2 hours.

4. The dough can be used immediately after the initial rise, though it is easier to handle when cold. Refrigerate it in a lidded (not airtight) container and use over the next 5 days. Or freeze for up to 4 weeks in 1-pound portions and thaw in the refrigerator overnight before use.

5. **On baking day:** Prepare a 6½-inch *banneton/brotform* by generously sprinkling it with flour; shake it all around so it coats the sides. Be generous with the flour. Dust the surface of the dough with rice flour and pull off a 1-pound (grapefruit-size) piece. This dough does not stretch, so quickly shape it into a ball, gently smoothing with flour-dusted fingers. Place the loaf into the *banneton*, with the smooth side in contact with the basket. Cover the *banneton* loosely with plastic wrap and allow to rest at room temperature for 60 minutes (see sidebar in Master Recipe step 5, page 70).

6. **Preheat a baking stone near the middle of the oven to 450°F (20 to 30 minutes),** with an empty metal broiler tray on any shelf that won't interfere with rising bread.

7. After the dough is rested, gently use your fingers to be sure that it isn't sticking to the *banneton*. Don't dig way down or you may deflate the loaf. Gently turn the basket over onto your pizza peel

prepared with cornmeal (use plenty) or parchment paper; it should unmold and drop gently. If it doesn't, help it out with your fingers and make the best of it. It should be fine even if it deflates a bit, thanks to oven spring. Make ½-inch-deep slashes with a wet serrated bread knife, in a cross pattern, which will create a beautiful effect with the concentric circles of flour (see photo, page 102).

8. Slide the loaf onto the hot stone. Pour 1 cup of hot tap water into the broiler tray, and quickly close the oven door (see page 31 for steam alternatives). Bake for **about 45 minutes,** or until richly browned and firm. Smaller or larger loaves will require adjustments in resting and baking time.

9. Allow to cool on a rack before eating.

VARIATION: BUCKWHEAT

Substitute ½ cup buckwheat flour (3 ounces) for millet flour, and replace the whole, raw millet with raw kasha (toasted whole buckwheat). Mix, shape, and bake the dough as above.

Seeded 100% Whole Grain Bread

Seed-lovers rejoice! This is your bread.
Makes five 1-pound loaves

Ingredient	Volume (U.S.), flour packed into measuring cups	Weight (U.S.)	Weight (Metric)
Mixture #2: 100% Whole-Grain Gluten-Free Flour (see page 62)	6½ cups	2 pounds, 4 ounces	1,015 grams
Ground flax seed	2 tablespoons	0.5 ounce	15 grams
Poppy seeds	2 tablespoons	0.75 ounce	20 grams
Chia seeds	2 tablespoons	0.75 ounce	20 grams
Sesame seeds	¼ cup	1½ ounces	45 grams
Pepitas	½ cup	3 ounces	85 grams
Sunflower seeds	½ cup	3 ounces	85 grams
Xanthan gum[1]	2 teaspoons	—	—
Granulated yeast	1 tablespoon	0.35 ounce	10 grams
Kosher salt[2]	1 to 1½ tablespoons	0.6 to 0.9 ounce	17 to 25 grams
Lukewarm water (100°F or below)	4 cups	2 pounds	910 grams
Molasses, honey, or agave syrup	¼ cup	2½ ounces	70 grams
Large eggs	4	8 ounces	225 grams
Cornmeal or parchment paper, for the pizza peel			

[1]If you used psyllium instead of xanthan gum in Mixture #2, do not use xanthan gum here.
[2]Can decrease (see page 25)

1. **Mixing and storing the dough:** Whisk together the flours, grains, seeds, xanthan, yeast, and salt in a 5- to 6-quart bowl, or a lidded (not airtight) food container.

2. Add the water, molasses, and eggs, and mix with a spoon or a heavy-duty stand mixer fitted with the paddle attachment (see page 42).

3. Cover (not airtight), and allow to rest at room temperature until the dough rises, approximately 2 hours.

4. The dough can be used immediately after the initial rise, though it is easier to handle when cold. Refrigerate it in a lidded (not airtight) container and use over the next 5 days. Or freeze for up to 4 weeks in 1-pound portions and thaw in the refrigerator overnight before use.

5. **On baking day:** Pull off a 1-pound (grapefruit-size) piece of dough. Place it on a pizza peel prepared with cornmeal (use plenty) or parchment paper. Quickly shape it into a ball and smooth the surface by gently pressing and smoothing with wet fingers. Cover loosely with plastic wrap or an overturned bowl and allow to rest for 60 minutes (see sidebar in Master Recipe, page 70).

6. **Preheat a baking stone near the middle of the oven to 450°F (20 to 30 minutes),** with an empty metal broiler tray on any shelf that won't interfere with rising bread.

7. After the dough is rested, gently use your fingers to be sure that it isn't sticking to the *banneton*. Don't dig way down or you may

deflate the loaf. Gently turn the basket over onto your pizza peel prepared with cornmeal (use plenty) or parchment paper; it should unmold and drop gently. If it doesn't, help it out with your fingers and make the best of it. It should be fine even if it deflates a bit, thanks to oven spring. Make ½-inch-deep slashes with a wet serrated bread knife (see photos page 70), in a cross pattern, which will create a beautiful effect with the concentric circles of flour (see photo, page 102).

8. Slide the loaf onto the hot stone. Pour 1 cup of hot tap water into the broiler tray, and quickly close the oven door (see page 31 for steam alternatives). Bake for **about 45 minutes,** or until richly browned and firm. Smaller or larger loaves will require adjustments in resting and baking time.

9. Allow to cool on a rack before eating.

Deli-Style "Rye" (Without the Rye)

Making a gluten-free bread in the rye style was one of our great triumphs, yet it was one of the easiest tricks to pull off (see color photo). Why? One word: seeds. And especially caraway seeds, which have a very, very distinct taste that everyone associates with the flavor of rye. Rye flour has less gluten than wheat, but it's still off-limits if you're off gluten. The teff flour in Mixture #2 echoes the earthy, slightly bittersweet flavor of rye.

Along with the caraway seeds, which are part of the classic flavor, what sets this "rye" apart from other rustic breads is that there is no flour on the top crust (see step 7, page 98) instead, it's glazed with water, which serves the triple function of anchoring the caraway seeds, allowing the slashing knife to pass easily without sticking, and adding color to the crust. If you're pressed for time, you can use plain water.

Makes four loaves, slightly more than 1 pound each. The recipe is easily doubled or halved.

Ingredient	Volume (U.S.), flour packed into measuring cups	Weight (U.S.)	Weight (Metric)
Mixture #1: Gluten-Free All-Purpose Flour (see page 60)	5½ cups	1 pound, 14 ounces	850 grams
Mixture #2: 100% Whole-Grain Gluten-Free Flour (see page 62)	1½ cup	8 ounces	255 grams
Granulated yeast	1 tablespoon	0.35 ounce	10 grams

(continued)

Visit GFBreadIn5.com, where you'll find recipes, photos, videos, and instructional material.

Ingredient	Volume (U.S.), flour packed into measuring cups	Weight (U.S.)	Weight (Metric)
Kosher salt[1]	1 to 1½ tablespoons	0.6 to 0.9 ounce	17 to 25 grams
Sugar (optional)	2 tablespoons	1 ounce	30 grams
Caraway seeds	2 tablespoons, plus additional for sprinkling on top	½ ounce	15 grams
Lukewarm water (100°F or below)	4¼ cups	2 pounds, 2 ounces	965 grams
Water, for brushing the loaves			
Cornmeal or parchment paper, for the pizza peel			

[1]Can decrease (see page 25)

1. **Mixing and storing the dough:** Whisk together the flours, yeast, salt, sugar (if using), and 2 tablespoons of the seeds in a 5- to 6-quart bowl, or a lidded (not airtight) food container.

2. Add the water and mix with a spoon or a heavy-duty stand mixer fitted with the paddle attachment (see page 42).

3. Cover (not airtight), and allow to rest at room temperature until the dough rises, approximately 2 hours.

4. The dough can be used immediately after the initial rise, though it is easier to handle when cold. Refrigerate it in a lidded (not airtight) container and use over the next 7 days. Or freeze for up to 4 weeks in 1-pound portions and thaw in the refrigerator overnight before use.

5. **On baking day:** Pull off a 1-pound (grapefruit-size) piece of dough. Place it on a pizza peel prepared with cornmeal (use plenty) or parchment paper. This dough does not stretch, so quickly shape it into an oval (see Bâtard, page 77), gently smoothing with wet fingers. Cover loosely with plastic wrap or an overturned bowl and allow to rest for 60 minutes (see sidebar in Master Recipe, page 70).

6. **Preheat a baking stone near the middle of the oven to 450°F (20 to 30 minutes),** with an empty metal broiler tray on any shelf that won't interfere with rising bread.

7. Brush with water and sprinkle with additional seeds. Slash, about ½ inch deep, with a wet serrated bread knife (see photos page 70).

8. Slide the loaf onto the hot stone. Pour 1 cup of hot tap water into the broiler tray, and quickly close the oven door (see page 31 for steam alternatives). Bake for **about 45 minutes,** or until richly browned and firm. Smaller or larger loaves will require adjustments in resting and baking time.

9. Allow to cool on a rack before eating.

Caraway Swirl "Rye"

This bread will really appeal to caraway lovers. An extra jolt of caraway seeds is swirled through the bread, producing a beautiful and flavorful crunch (see color photo).

Makes 1 loaf

1 pound (grapefruit-size portion) Deli-Style "Rye" dough (page 109)
2 tablespoons caraway seeds, plus additional for sprinkling on the top
Water, for brushing the loaf
Parchment paper or a silicone mat, for shaping and baking

1. Dust the surface of the dough with rice flour and pull off a 1-pound (grapefruit-size) piece. Place it on a flour-dusted surface. Sprinkle the dough with more flour and press the dough with flour-dusted fingers until you have a ½-inch-thick rectangle. Check occasionally to be sure the dough is not sticking. If it is, carefully lift the stuck part of the dough and sprinkle more flour under it.

2. Distribute the 2 tablespoons of caraway seeds over the dough, reserving the rest for the top crust. Roll the dough, starting on the long side, into a log. Place the log on parchment and smooth the surface with wet fingers. Cover loosly with plastic and allow to rest for 60 minutes.

3. **Preheat a baking stone near the middle of the oven to 450°F (20 to 30 minutes),** with an empty metal broiler tray on any shelf that won't interfere with rising bread.

4. Brush the top with water and sprinkle with additional caraway seeds. Slash with ½-inch-deep parallel cuts across the loaf, using a wet serrated bread knife.

5. Slide the loaf onto the hot stone. Pour 1 cup of hot tap water into the broiler tray, and quickly close the oven door (see page 31 for steam alternatives). Bake for **about 45 minutes,** or until richly browned and firm. Smaller or larger loaves will require adjustments in resting and baking time.

6. Allow to cool on a rack before eating.

Onion "Rye"

The homey, comforting flavor of sautéed onion is one of life's simplest and most satisfying pleasures, especially when combined with hearty rye bread. Be sure to brown the onion to achieve the caramelization that makes this bread so savory. This recipe can be made with or without caraway seeds. Ordinary yellow or white onions work well and are readily available, but Vidalia or red varieties produce a milder onion flavor that some may prefer.

Makes 1 loaf

1 pound (grapefruit-size portion) Deli-Style "Rye" dough (page 109)
1 medium onion, halved and thinly sliced
Vegetable oil, for sautéing the onions
Cornmeal or parchment paper, for the pizza peel
Caraway seeds (optional)
Parchment paper or a silicone mat, for shaping and baking
Water for brushing the loaf

1. Sauté the sliced onion in the oil over medium heat in a skillet for 10 minutes, or until brown and nicely caramelized.

2. Dust the surface of the refrigerated dough with rice flour and pull off a 1-pound (grapefruit-size) piece. Place it on a piece of parchment paper or a silicone mat prepared with flour. Sprinkle the dough with more flour and press the dough with flour-dusted fingers until you have a ½-inch-thick rectangle. Check occasionally to be sure the dough is not sticking to the parchment. If it is,

carefully lift the stuck part of the dough and sprinkle more flour under it.

3. Distribute the browned onion over the dough, reserving some for the top crust. Roll the dough, starting on the long side, into a log, lifting the parchment paper to help ease the dough from its surface. Be sure that the seam is at the bottom of the loaf. Smooth the surface with wet fingers. Cover loosely with plastic and allow to rest for 60 minutes.

4. **Preheat a baking stone near the middle of the oven to 450°F (20 to 30 minutes),** with an empty metal broiler tray on any shelf that won't interfere with rising bread.

5. Brush the top with water, and then sprinkle with the caraway seeds (if using). Slash with $\frac{1}{2}$-inch-deep parallel cuts across the loaf, using a wet serrated bread knife (see photos, page 70).

6. Slide the loaf onto the hot stone. Pour 1 cup of hot tap water into the broiler tray, and quickly close the oven door (see page 31 for steam alternatives). Bake for **about 45 minutes,** or until richly browned and firm. Smaller or larger loaves will require adjustments in resting and baking time.

7. Allow to cool on a rack before eating.

Seeded Flaxen Loaf

Sesame seeds are a wonderful complement to the flavor of ground flax-seeds in this slightly sweet, nutty loaf. It's fabulous with jam or cheese for breakfast.

Makes four loaves, slightly more than 1 pound each. The recipe is easily doubled or halved.

Ingredient	Volume (U.S.), flour packed into measuring cups	Weight (U.S.)	Weight (Metric)
Mixture #1: Gluten-Free All-Purpose Flour (see page 60)	6½ cups	2 pounds, 3 ounces	985 grams
Flaxseed, ground	½ cup	2½ ounces	70 grams
Granulated yeast	1 tablespoon	0.35 ounce	10 grams
Kosher salt[1]	1 to 1½ tablespoons	0.6 to 0.9 ounce	17 to 25 grams
Sesame seeds	¼ cup, plus additional for sprinkling the top	1¼ ounces	35 grams
Sugar (optional)	2 tablespoons	1 ounce	30 grams
Lukewarm water (100°F or below)	4 cups	2 pounds	910 grams
Honey	⅓ cup	4 ounces	115 grams
Cornmeal or parchment paper, for the pizza peel			
Top-crust wash or water, for brushing the loaves			

[1]Can decrease (see page 25)

1. **Mixing and storing the dough:** Whisk together the flour, flaxseed, yeast, salt, 1/4 cup sesame seeds, and sugar (if using) in a 5- to 6-quart bowl, or a lidded (not airtight) food container.

2. Add the liquid ingredients and mix with a spoon or a heavy-duty stand mixer fitted with the paddle attachment (see page 42).

3. Cover (not airtight), and allow to rest at room temperature until the dough rises, approximately 2 hours.

4. The dough can be used immediately after the initial rise, though it is easier to handle when cold. Refrigerate it in a lidded (not airtight) container and use over the next 10 days. Or freeze for up to 4 weeks in 1-pound portions and thaw in the refrigerator overnight before use.

5. **On baking day:** Pull off a 1-pound (grapefruit-size) piece of dough. Place it on a pizza peel prepared with cornmeal (use plenty) or parchment paper. Quickly shape it into a ball and smooth the surface by gently pressing and smoothing with wet fingers. Cover loosely with plastic wrap or an overturned bowl and allow to rest for 60 minutes (see sidebar in Master Recipe, page 70).

6. **Preheat a baking stone near the middle of the oven to 450°F (20 to 30 minutes),** with an empty metal broiler tray on any shelf that won't interfere with rising bread.

7. Brush with water, sprinkle with additional sesame seeds, and slash, about 1/2 inch deep, with a wet serrated bread knife (see photos, page 70).

8. Slide the loaf onto the hot stone. Pour 1 cup of hot tap water into the broiler tray, and quickly close the oven door (see page 31 for steam alternatives). Bake for **about 45 minutes,** or until richly browned and firm. Smaller or larger loaves will require adjustments in resting and baking time.

9. Allow to cool on a rack before eating.

Almond Coconut Loaf

Many of our readers have asked us for recipes that replace some of the grain found in bread with nut flours—nuts have a lower glycemic index than starchy grains (they increase blood glucose more slowly, and to a lesser degree). We love the rich flavor of coconut flour and almond meal, and they work beautifully in yeasted dough.

Makes four 1-pound loaves. The recipe is easily doubled or halved.

Ingredient	Volume (U.S.), flour packed into measuring cups	Weight (U.S.)	Weight (Metric)
Mixture #1: Gluten-Free All-Purpose Flour (see page 60)	4½ cups	1 pound, 9 ounces	700 grams
Coconut flour	¾ cup	3¾ ounces	105 grams
Shredded unsweetened coconut	½ cup	1½ ounces	45 grams
Almond meal	1½ cups	8 ounces	225 grams
Xanthan gum or ground psyllium husk[1]	2 teaspoons	—	—
Granulated yeast	1 tablespoon	0.35 ounce	10 grams
Kosher salt[2]	1 to 1½ tablespoons	0.6–0.9 ounce	17–25 grams
Lukewarm water (100°F or below)	4¼ cups	2 pounds, 2 ounces	965 grams
Honey	½ cup	6 ounces	170 grams
Cornmeal or parchment paper, for the pizza peel			

[1]Double quantity if using psyllium
[2]Can decrease (see page 25)

---

1. **Mixing and storing the dough:** Whisk together the flours, shreddded coconut, almond meal, xanthan gum, yeast, and salt in the bowl of a stand mixer or in any 5-quart bowl, or any lidded (not airtight) food container.

2. Add the liquid ingredients and mix with a spoon or a heavy-duty stand mixer fitted with the paddle attachment (see page 42).

3. Cover (not airtight), and allow to rest at room temperature until the dough rises, approximately 2 hours.

4. The dough can be used immediately after the initial rise, though it is easier to handle when cold. Refrigerate it in a lidded (not airtight) container and use over the next 5 days. Or freeze for up to 3 weeks in 1-pound portions and thaw in the refrigerator overnight before use.

5. **On baking day:** Pull off a 1-pound (grapefruit-size) piece of dough. Place it on a pizza peel prepared with cornmeal (use plenty) or parchment paper. Quickly shape it into a ball, gently pressing and smoothing with wet fingers. Cover loosely with plastic wrap or an overturned bowl and allow to rest for 60 minutes (see sidebar in Master Recipe, page 70).

6. **Preheat a baking stone near the middle of the oven to 450°F (20 to 30 minutes),** with an empty metal broiler tray on any shelf that won't interfere with rising bread.

7. Dust the top with rice flour and slash, about ½ inch deep, with a
    wet serrated bread knife (see photos, page 70).

8. Slide the loaf onto the hot stone. Pour 1 cup of hot tap water into
    the broiler tray, and quickly close the oven door (see page 31 for
    steam alternatives). Bake for **about 45 minutes,** or until richly
    browned and firm. Smaller or larger loaves will require adjustments
    in resting and baking time.

9. Allow to cool on a rack before eating.

Olive Oil Dough and Olive Bread

Adding zesty flavors perks up the flavor of gluten-free breads, and there's nothing quite so zesty as olives to remind us of the Mediterranean from where this bread comes. It's great in pizza and flatbreads, or baked into any of the shapes we covered in Chapter 6. This recipe also introduces a technique that allows you to incorporate flavorful ingredients into a single loaf if you want to get different kinds of bread from a single batch of dough.

Makes at least three 1-pound loaves. The recipe is easily doubled or halved.

Ingredient	Volume (U.S.), flour packed into measuring cups	Weight (U.S.)	Weight (Metric)
Mixture #1: Gluten-Free All-Purpose Flour (see page 60)	6 cups	2 pounds	910 grams
Granulated yeast	1 tablespoon	0.35 ounce	10 grams
Kosher salt[1]	1 to 1½ tablespoons	0.6 to 0.9 ounce	17 to 25 grams
Sugar (optional)	2 tablespoons	1 ounce	30 grams
Lukewarm water (100°F or below)	3¼ cups	1 pound, 10 ounces	740 grams
Olive oil	¼ cup	2 ounces	55 grams
Cornmeal or parchment paper, for the pizza peel			
Water, for brushing the loaves			

[1]Can decrease (see page 25)

1. **Mixing and storing the dough:** Whisk together the flour, yeast, salt, and sugar (if using) in a 5- to 6-quart bowl, or a lidded (not airtight) food container.

2. Add the liquid ingredients and mix with a spoon or a heavy-duty stand mixer fitted with the paddle attachment (see page 42).

3. Cover (not airtight), and allow to rest at room temperature until the dough rises, approximately 2 hours.

4. The dough can be used immediately after the initial rise, though it is easier to handle when cold. Refrigerate it in a lidded (not airtight) container and use over the next 7 days. Or freeze for up to 4 weeks in 1-pound portions and thaw in the refrigerator overnight before use.

5. **On baking day:** Pull off a 1-pound (grapefruit-size) piece of dough. Place it on a pizza peel prepared with cornmeal (use plenty) or parchment paper. Quickly shape it into a ball and smooth the surface by gently pressing and smoothing with wet fingers. Cover loosely with plastic wrap or an overturned bowl and allow to rest for 60 minutes (see sidebar in Master Recipe, page 70).

6. **Preheat a baking stone near the middle of the oven to 450°F (20 to 30 minutes),** with an empty metal broiler tray on any shelf that won't interfere with rising bread.

7. Brush the top with water, and then slash, about ½ inch deep, with a wet serrated bread knife (see photos, page 70).

8. Slide the loaf onto the hot stone. Pour 1 cup of hot tap water into the broiler tray, and quickly close the oven door (see page 31 for steam alternatives). Bake for **about 45 minutes,** or until richly browned and firm. Smaller or larger loaves will require adjustments in resting and baking time.

9. Allow to cool on a rack before eating.

VARIATION: OLIVE BREAD (Use Any Dough and Roll Olives into a Single Loaf)

Good black or green olives impart fabulous flavor and texture to peasant loaves. You can make olive bread from plain doughs by incorporating halved olives into a 1-pound (grapefruit-size portion) of any lean dough (any dough other than those in Chapter 9). Here's how:

1. Dust the surface of the dough with rice flour and pull off a 1-pound (grapefruit-size) piece. Place it on a flour-dusted surface. Sprinkle the dough with more flour and press the dough with flour-dusted fingers until you have a ½-inch-thick rectangle. Check occasionally to be sure the dough is not sticking. If it is, carefully lift the stuck part of the dough and sprinkle more flour under it.

2. Distribute ¼ cup of halved, pitted olives over the dough. Roll the dough, starting on the long side, into a log. Place the log on parchment paper, smooth with wet fingers, cover loosely with plastic wrap, and allow to rest for 60 minutes. See page 132 for photos of roll-in technique.

3. Continue from Step 6 on page 123.

Limpa

Limpa is so traditional in the Scandinavian countries that it's a bit scary to mess with it. But really, it's the spices, honey, and orange zest that make it limpa, so we saw no reason that our gluten-free friends shouldn't get to eat this fantastic treat, with its exotic flavors of anise and cardamom.

Makes five 1-pound loaves. The recipe is easily doubled or halved.

Ingredient	Volume (U.S.), flour packed into measuring cups	Weight (U.S.)	Weight (Metric)
Mixture #1: Gluten-Free All-Purpose Flour (see page 60)	6 cups	2 pounds	910 grams
Mixture #2: 100% Whole-Grain Gluten-Free Flour (see page 62)	1 cup	5½ ounces	155 grams
Granulated yeast	1 tablespoon	0.35 ounce	10 grams
Kosher salt[1]	1 to 1½ tablespoons	0.6 to 0.9 ounce	17 to 25 grams
Anise seed, ground	½ teaspoon	—	—
Cardamom, ground	1 teaspoon	—	—
Orange zest (see Equipment, page 43)	1½ teaspoons	—	—

[1]Can decrease (see page 25)

(continued)

Visit GFBreadIn5.com, where you'll find recipes, photos, videos, and instructional material.

Ingredient	Volume (U.S.), flour packed into measuring cups	Weight (U.S.)	Weight (Metric)
Lukewarm water (100°F or below)	4 cups	2 pounds	910 grams
Honey	½ cup	6 ounces	170 grams
Spiced sugar for each loaf: mix together ¼ teaspoon ground anise seed, ¼ ground cardamom, and 1½ teaspoons sugar			
Cornmeal or parchment paper, for the pizza peel			
Water, for brushing the loaves			

1. **Mixing and storing the dough:** Whisk together the flours, yeast, salt, ground seeds, cardamom, and zest in the bowl of a stand mixer or in a 5-quart bowl, or any lidded (not airtight) food container.

2. Add the liquid ingredients and mix with a spoon or a heavy-duty stand mixer fitted with the paddle attachment (see page 42).

3. Cover (not airtight), and allow to rest at room temperature until the dough rises, approximately 2 hours.

4. The dough can be used immediately after the initial rise, though it is easier to handle when cold. Refrigerate the container of dough and use over the next 7 days.

5. Pull off a 1-pound (grapefruit-size) piece of dough. Place it on a pizza peel prepared with cornmeal (use plenty) or parchment paper. Quickly shape it into a ball and smooth the surface by gently

pressing and smoothing with wet fingers. Cover loosely with plastic wrap or an overturned bowl and allow to rest for 60 minutes (see sidebar in Master Recipe, page 70).

6. **Preheat a baking stone near the middle of the oven to 400°F (20 to 30 minutes),** with an empty metal broiler tray on any shelf that won't interfere with rising bread.

7. Brush the top with water, sprinkle with spiced sugar mixture, and then slash the top, about ½ inch deep, using a serrated bread knife (see photos, page 70). Sprinkle with the spiced-sugar mixture.

8. Slide the loaf directly onto the hot stone. Pour 1 cup of hot tap water into the broiler tray, and quickly close the oven door (see page 31 for steam alternatives). Bake for **about 45 minutes,** or until golden brown and firm. Smaller or larger loaves will require adjustments in baking time. Due to the honey in the recipe, the crust on this bread will not be hard and crackling.

9. Allow to cool on a rack before eating.

"Pumpernickel" Bread

Pumpernickel bread is really just a variety of "rye" bread. What darkens the loaf and accounts for its mildly bitter but appealing flavor is powdered caramel coloring, cocoa powder, molasses, and coffee, not the flour. The caramel color is actually a natural ingredient made by overheating sugar until it is completely caramelized (available as a powder from King Arthur Flour; see Sources for Bread-Baking Products, page 274, or see the sidebar on page 130 to make your own liquid version). Since it's really the caramel, coffee, and chocolate that give pumpernickel its unique flavor and color, we successfully created a gluten-free pumpernickel bread *without* pumpernickel flour.

This bread is often associated with Russia and caviar. Or just pile on the pastrami and corned beef.

Makes four 1-pound loaves. The recipe is easily doubled or halved.

Ingredient	Volume (U.S.), flour packed into measuring cups	Weight (U.S.)	Weight (Metric)
Mixture #1: Gluten-Free All-Purpose Flour (see page 60)	6 cups	2 pounds	910 grams
Mixture #2: 100% Whole-Grain Gluten-Free Flour (see page 62)	1 cup	5½ ounces	155 grams
Cocoa powder, unsweetened	1½ tablespoons	0.4 ounce	10 grams

(continued)

Ingredient	Volume (U.S.), flour packed into measuring cups	Weight (U.S.)	Weight (Metric)
Instant espresso or instant coffee powder	2 teaspoons	—	—
Caramel color powder	2 tablespoons	—	—
Granulated yeast	1 tablespoon	0.35 ounce	10 grams
Kosher salt[1]	1 to 1½ tablespoons	0.6 to 0.9 ounce	17 to 25 grams
Lukewarm water (100°F or below)[2]	4 cups	2 pounds	910 grams
Molasses	2 tablespoons	1¼ ounces	35 grams
Parchment paper or a silicone mat, for the pizza peel			
Water, for brushing the loaves			
Caraway seeds, for sprinkling on the top (optional)			

[1]Can decrease (see page 25)
[2]Can substitute brewed coffee for 2 cups of the water, keeping total volume at 4 cups

∽

Make your own caramel color: Caramel color can be made at home, but as a liquid rather than a powder. Put 3 tablespoons sugar and 1 tablespoon water into a saucepan. Over high heat, melt the sugar and boil, uncovered, until the mixture becomes very dark. Remove from heat. Very carefully, add ¼ cup of boiling water to the pan to dissolve the caramelized sugar (it may sputter and water may jump out of the pan so wear gloves and be sure to shield your face). Cool to room temperature and use about ¼ cup of this mixture in place of the 2 tablespoons of commercial caramel color powder in our Pumpernickel Bread (decrease the water in your initial mix by ¼ cup).

1. **Mixing and storing the dough:** Whisk together the flours, cocoa powder, espresso/coffee powder, caramel color, yeast, and salt in a 5- to 6-quart bowl, or a lidded (not airtight) food container.

2. Add the liquid ingredients and mix with a spoon or a heavy-duty stand mixer fitted with the attachment (see page 42).

3. Cover (not airtight), and allow to rest at room temperature until the dough rises and collapses (or flattens on top), approximately 2 hours.

4. The dough can be used immediately after the initial rise, though it is easier to handle when cold. Refrigerate the container of dough and use over the next 5 days, or freeze for up to 4 weeks.

5. **On baking day:** Using wet hands, pull off a 1-pound (grapefruit-size) piece of dough and place it on a pizza peel lined with parchment paper or a silicone mat. Quickly shape it into an oval (see Bâtard, page 77), and smooth the surface by gently pressing with wet hands. Cover loosely with plastic wrap or an overturned bowl and allow to rest for 60 minutes (see sidebar in Master Recipe, page 70).

6. **Preheat a baking stone near the middle of the oven to 425°F (20 to 30 minutes),** with an empty metal broiler tray on any shelf that won't interfere with rising bread.

7. Brush the top with water, and then sprinkle with the caraway seeds (if using). Slash the loaf with ½-inch-deep, parallel cuts, using a wet serrated bread knife (see photo page 76).

8. Slide the loaf directly onto the hot stone. Pour 1 cup of hot tap water into the broiler tray, and quickly close the oven door (see page 31 for steam alternatives). Bake for **45 minutes,** until firm. Smaller or larger loaves will require adjustments in baking time.

9. Allow to cool on a rack before eating.

"Pumpernickel" Date-and-Walnut Bread

The sweetness of the dried fruit and the richness of the nuts are wonderful with the aromatic pumpernickel dough. Even though pumpernickel's an assertive flavor, the fruit and nuts take center stage.

Makes 1 loaf

1 pound (grapefruit-size portion) Pumpernickel Bread dough (page 128)
¼ cup chopped walnuts
¼ cup chopped dates or raisins
Parchment paper or a silicone mat, for the pizza peel
Water, for brushing the loaf

1. Dust the surface of the dough with rice flour and pull out a 1-pound (grapefruit-size) piece. Place it on a piece of parchment paper or a silicone mat prepared with flour. Sprinkle the dough with more flour and press the dough until you have a ½-inch-thick rectangle. Check occasionally to be sure the dough is not sticking to the parchment paper. If it is, carefully lift the stuck part of the dough and sprinkle more flour under it.

2. Distribute the walnuts and fruit over the dough. Roll the dough, starting on the long side, into a log, lifting the parchment paper or silicone mat

to help ease the dough from its surface. Smooth the log with wet fingers, cover loosely with plastic, and allow to rest for 60 minutes.

3. **Preheat a baking stone near the middle of the oven to 400°F (20 to 30 minutes),** with an empty metal broiler tray on any shelf that won't interfere with rising bread.

4. Brush the top with water, and then slash, about ½ inch deep, with a wet serrated bread knife (see photos, page 70).

5. Slide the loaf (or place the silicone mat) onto the hot stone. Pour 1 cup of hot tap water into the broiler tray, and quickly close the oven door (see page 31 for steam alternatives). Bake for **about 50 minutes,** or until richly browned and firm. Smaller or larger loaves will require adjustments in resting and baking time.

6. Allow to cool on a rack before eating.

Oat Bran–Enriched White Bread

We've used wheat bran to pump up the fiber content of ordinary white bread, and the same principle holds here. For folks who don't like whole-grain breads, you can still deliver more fiber just by using bran. But you can't use wheat bran—it's not gluten-free! Enter oat bran.

We talked about the controversies around oats in Chapter 2 (see page 9), but most experts agree that even celiacs can eat up to ½ cup of oatmeal a day, let alone oat bran, which excludes most of the protein and starch portions of the oat kernel. If you have any doubt, check with your doctor.

Makes about four 1-pound loaves

Ingredient	Volume (U.S.), flour packed into measuring cups	Weight (U.S.)	Weight (Metric)
Mixture #1: Gluten-Free All-Purpose Flour (see page 60)	5¾ cups	1 pound, 15 ounces	870 grams
Oat flour	½ cup	2¼ ounces	65 grams
Oat bran	¾ cup	3¼ ounces	90 grams
Granulated yeast	1 tablespoon	0.35 ounce	10 grams
Kosher salt[1]	1 to 1½ tablespoons	0.6 to 0.9 ounce	17 to 25 grams
Sugar (optional)	2 tablespoons	1 ounce	30 grams
Lukewarm water (100°F or below)	4¼ cups	2 pounds, 2 ounces	965 grams
Cornmeal or parchment paper, for the pizza peel			

[1]Can decrease (see page 25)

1. **Mixing and storing the dough:** Whisk together the flour, bran, yeast, salt, and sugar (if using) in a 5- to 6-quart bowl, or a lidded (not airtight) food container.

2. Add the water and mix with a spoon or a heavy-duty stand mixer fitted with the paddle attachment (see page 42).

3. Cover (not airtight), and allow to rest at room temperature until the dough rises, approximately 2 hours.

4. The dough can be used immediately after the initial rise, though it is easier to handle when cold. Refrigerate it in a lidded (not airtight) container and use over the next 10 days. Or freeze for up to 4 weeks in 1-pound portions and thaw in the refrigerator overnight before use.

5. **On baking day:** Pull off a 1-pound (grapefruit-size) piece of dough. Place it on a pizza peel prepared with cornmeal (use plenty), or parchment paper. Quickly shape it into a ball and smooth the surface by gently pressing and smoothing with wet fingers. Cover loosely with plastic wrap or an overturned bowl and allow to rest for 60 minutes (see sidebar in Master Recipe, page 70).

6. **Preheat a baking stone near the middle of the oven to 450°F (20 to 30 minutes),** with an empty metal broiler tray on any shelf that won't interfere with rising bread.

7. Dust the top with rice flour and slash, about ½ inch deep, with a wet serrated bread knife (see photos, page 70).

8. Slide the loaf onto the hot stone. Pour 1 cup of hot tap water into the broiler tray, and quickly close the oven door (see page 31 for steam alternatives). Bake for **about 45 minutes,** or until richly browned and firm. Smaller or larger loaves will require adjustments in resting and baking time.

9. Allow to cool on a rack before eating

Broa (Portuguese Cornbread)

Broa is a very rustic bread recipe from the Portuguese countryside (see color photo). It's a dense, part-corn loaf that's perfect for sopping up hearty soups, which is how it's used in Portugal. Unlike American Southern cornbread, it's not sweetened, and it's leavened with yeast, not baking soda and powder. The corn really carries the day here, and it's very, very hard to tell this from the wheat version.

Form this loaf as a relatively flattened ball, so that you'll get lots of crust. The flattened loaf is truer to the original and helps to prevent denseness from the corn.

Makes four 1-pound loaves. The recipe is easily doubled or halved.

Ingredient	Volume (U.S.), flour packed into measuring cups	Weight (U.S.)	Weight (Metric)
Mixture #1: Gluten-Free All-Purpose Flour (see page 60)	5 cups	1 pound, 12 ounces	780 grams
Cornmeal, plus more for dusting the loaf	1½ cups	9 ounces	255 grams
Granulated yeast	1 tablespoon	0.35 ounce	10 grams
Kosher salt[1]	1 to 1½ tablespoons	0.6 ounce	17 grams
Sugar (optional)	2 tablespoons	1 ounce	30 grams
Lukewarm water (100°F or below)	4¼ cups	2 pounds, 2 ounces	965 grams
Cornmeal or parchment paper, for the pizza peel			

[1]Can decrease (see page 25)

1. **Mixing and storing the dough:** Whisk together the flour, cornmeal, yeast, salt and sugar (if using) in a 5- to 6-quart bowl, or a lidded (not airtight) food container.

2. Add the water and mix with a spoon or a heavy-duty stand mixer fitted with the paddle attachment (see page 42).

3. Cover (not airtight), and allow to rest at room temperature until the dough rises, approximately 2 hours.

4. The dough can be used immediately after the initial rise, though it is easier to handle when cold. Refrigerate it in a lidded (not airtight) container and use over the next 10 days. Or freeze for up to 4 weeks in 1-pound portions and thaw in the refrigerator overnight before use.

5. **On baking day:** Pull off a 1-pound (grapefruit-size) piece of dough. Place it on a pizza peel prepared with parchment paper or cornmeal (use plenty). Quickly shape it into a flattened ball and smooth the surface by gently pressing with wet hands. Cover loosely with plastic wrap or an overturned bowl and allow to rest for 60 minutes (see sidebar in Master Recipe, page 70).

6. **Preheat a baking stone near the middle of the oven to 450°F (20 to 30 minutes),** with an empty metal broiler tray on any shelf that won't interfere with rising bread.

7. Sprinkle the top with cornmeal and slash, about ½ inch deep, with a wet serrated bread knife (see photos, page 70).

8. Slide the loaf onto the hot stone. Pour 1 cup of hot tap water into the broiler tray, and quickly close the oven door (see page 31 for steam alternatives). Bake for **about 45 minutes,** or until richly browned and firm. Smaller or larger loaves will require adjustments in resting and baking time.

9. Allow to cool slightly on a rack before cutting into wedges.

Yeasted Thanksgiving Cornbread with Cranberries

Traditional American cornbread is a butter- or lard-enriched quick bread with corn and wheat, risen with baking powder and baking soda (see color photo). Our version has less sweetener and is leavened with yeast. Thanksgiving means cranberries, so we studded the Broa dough (page 137) with them. In the classic American cornbread style, we baked the loaf in a heated cast-iron pan, liberally greased with butter, lard, bacon grease, or oil, creating a rich and flavorful crust. The cast-iron pan browns the crust beautifully.

Makes 1 loaf

1 pound (grapefruit-size portion) Broa dough (page 137), or enough to fill an
    8-inch cast-iron pan to a depth of about 1 inch
½ cup fresh cranberries, or ⅓ cup dried cranberries
¼ cup sugar
Zest of ½ orange
1 tablespoon softened butter, lard, bacon grease, or oil, for greasing the pan

1. Grease a cast-iron pan with the butter, lard, bacon grease, or oil, being sure to coat the sides of the pan as well. Set aside.

2. Pull off a 1-pound (grapefruit-size) piece of dough and quickly shape it into a ball.

3. Place the dough into the prepared pan and press it to the edges. Cover the dough with the cranberries, sugar, and orange zest,

pressing the berries into the dough. Cover with plastic wrap or the pan's lid and allow the dough to rest for 45 minutes (see sidebar in Master Recipe, step 5, page 70).

4. **Preheat the oven to 450°F.** (A baking stone is not required, and omitting it shortens the preheat.)

5. Uncover the pan and place it on a rack near the middle of the oven. **Check for browning in about 20 to 25 minutes.** The total time required will depend on the size and weight of the pan, but will probably be **25 to 30 minutes.** The loaf should be a rich golden brown when done.

6. Carefully turn the hot loaf out of the pan onto a serving plate, or just cut wedges directly from the pan.

Spicy Pork Buns

Southern Mexico is a great place to start gluten-free recipe explorations, because the grain of choice there is corn, not wheat. Unlike the north of Mexico and the United States, where "flour" (white wheat) tortillas rule the food trucks, chefs of southern Mexico make wonderful things from *masa*, which is a corn dough—think corn tortillas and tamales. Our Broa dough (page 137) fits the bill, and when you combine it with a Mexican-style meat filling, you can re-create some of the great flavors of a corn tamale (if you don't eat pork you can substitute beef brisket). If you don't love spicy food, tone down the *chipotles en adobo* (which are the really hot ones), or leave them out entirely. We serve this dish as a main course, with extra sauce on the side. You can put more sauce inside the buns, but don't overdo it or the buns may be soggy (see color photo).

Makes 4 large buns

The Meat Filling

2 dried chile peppers (New Mexico red, *guajillo*, or ancho variety), or substitute
   1 tablespoon of your favorite chile powder

1½ teaspoons cumin seeds

4 to 5 pounds pork roast (shoulder or butt) or beef brisket

One 28-ounce can crushed tomatoes

2 chipotle peppers from a can of *chipotles en adobo*, finely chopped

1 medium onion, coarsely chopped

2 teaspoons salt

1 tablespoon cornstarch

2 tablespoons chopped fresh cilantro

The Wrappers

1 pound (grapefruit-size portion) *Broa* dough (page 137), or other lean dough
    (any dough other than those in Chapter 9)

Water, for brushing the buns

1. **Prepare the meat filling:** If you're grinding your own chile pepper, briefly toast the dried peppers in a 400°F oven until fragrant but not burned, 1 to 2 minutes (they'll remain flexible). Break up the toasted peppers and discard the stems and seeds. Grind with the cumin seeds in a spice grinder (or a coffee grinder used just for spices).

2. Place all the ingredients for the meat filling except the cornstarch and cilantro in a roomy pot on the stovetop; the pot should be large enough to hold the meat and still allow the cover to seal. The liquid should not come higher than about one-third of the way up the meat. Bring to a simmer and cook, covered, until very soft, approximately 3 hours, turning occasionally. Separate the meat and sauce and chill in the refrigerator.

3. Trim the meat of hardened fat; shred with a knife, fork, and your fingers, pulling strips off the roast or brisket along the direction of the grain. You'll have plenty of meat left over for additional buns or other meals.

4. Skim the fat from the surface of the sauce. Anytime before assembling the buns, reheat the meat mixture. Mix the cornstarch with a small amount of sauce in a little cup to make a paste; add to the pot. Simmer for 2 minutes, or until thickened.

5. **Preheat a baking stone near the middle of the oven to 450°F (20 to 30 minutes),** with an empty metal broiler tray on any shelf that won't interfere with rising bread.

6. Dust the surface of the dough with rice flour and pull off a 1-pound (grapefruit-size) piece. Divide the dough into four equal pieces and quickly pat each into a ball on a work surface prepared with rice flour. Smooth the surface and flatten into a disk by gently pressing with your fingers, until you reach a thickness of ⅛ inch (8- to 10-inch rounds). Check to be sure that the dough isn't sticking and, if it is, lift and dust with more flour. As you work, pat the sides to round them off.

7. **Assemble the buns:** Place about 3 tablespoons of shredded meat in the center of each round of dough. Add about a tablespoon of sauce and ½ tablespoon of chopped cilantro to each. Wet the edges of the dough round with water. Gather the edges of the dough around the meat to form a pouch, pinching at the center to seal.

8. Using a dough scraper if necessary, remove the finished buns from the work surface and place on a cornmeal-covered pizza peel. No resting time is needed. Brush lightly with water.

9. Slide the buns directly onto the hot stone. Pour 1 cup of hot tap water into the broiler tray, and quickly close the oven door (see page 31 for steam alternatives). **Check for browning in 15 minutes,** and continue baking until the buns are medium brown, probably 20 to 25 minutes.

10. Serve immediately, with additional sauce and if desired, Mexican hot pepper sauce.

Oatmeal Maple Bread

This high-fiber loaf is sweetened with maple syrup and tastes great cut into thick slices and then slathered with butter. It also makes a great sandwich with smoked turkey and cheese (see color photo).

Makes two 2-pound loaves. The recipe is easily doubled or halved.

Ingredient	Volume (U.S.), flour packed into measuring cups	Weight (U.S.)	Weight (Metric)
Mixture #1: Gluten-Free All-Purpose Flour (see page 60)	4½ cups	1 pound, 8 ounces	680 grams
Oat flour	½ cup	2¼ ounces	65 grams
Old-fashioned rolled oats, plus additional for sprinkling	2½ cups	8 ounces	225 grams
Granulated yeast	1 tablespoon	0.35 ounce	10 grams
Kosher salt[1]	1 to 1½ tablespoons	0.6 to 0.9 ounce	17 to 25 grams
Lukewarm water (100°F or below)	3¼ cups	1 pound, 10 ounces	740 grams
Maple syrup	1 cup, plus 1 tablespoon for brushing the top	8 ounces	225 grams

[1]Can decrease (see page 25)

1. **Mixing and storing the dough:** Whisk together the flour, oats, yeast, and salt in a 5- to 6-quart bowl, or a lidded (not airtight) food container.

2. Add the water and 1 cup of the maple syrup and mix with a spoon
   or a heavy-duty stand mixer fitted with the paddle attachment (see
   page 42).

3. Cover (not airtight), and allow to rest at room temperature until
   the dough rises, approximately 2 hours.

4. The dough can be used immediately after the initial rise, though
   it is easier to handle when cold. Refrigerate it in a lidded (not
   airtight) container and use over the next 5 days. Or freeze for up to
   4 weeks in 1-pound portions and thaw in the refrigerator overnight
   before use.

5. **On baking day,** grease an 8½ × 4½-inch nonstick loaf pan. Using
   wet hands, pull off a 2-pound (cantaloupe-size) piece of dough,
   quickly shape it into a ball, and smooth the surface by gently
   pressing with wet hands. Elongate the ball into an oval and drop it
   into the prepared pan. Smooth the surface with wet fingers.

6. Cover loosely with plastic wrap or an overturned bowl and allow to
   rest for 90 minutes (see sidebar in Master Recipe step 5, page 70).

7. **Preheat the oven to 400°F.**

8. Brush with 1 tablespoon of the maple syrup and sprinkle with oats,
   then slash, about ½ inch deep, with a wet serrated bread knife (see
   photos, page 70).

9. Put the pan in the oven on a middle shelf, pour 1 cup of hot tap
   water into the broiler tray, and quickly close the oven door (see

page 31 for steam alternatives). Bake for **55 to 60 minutes,** or until richly browned and firm. Smaller or larger loaves will require adjustments in resting and baking time.

10. Remove the loaf from the pan and allow to cool completely on a rack before slicing; otherwise, you won't get well-cut slices. If the loaf sticks, wait 10 minutes and it will steam itself out of the pan.

Raisin-Walnut Oatmeal Bread

Full of the flavors we associate with oatmeal—raisins, walnuts, and a touch of maple syrup—this will remind you of the breakfast your mother made you when you were a kid. If not, it will be the breakfast your kids beg you to make (see color photo).

Makes 1 loaf

Oil, for greasing the pan

1½ pounds (small cantaloupe–size portion) Oatmeal Maple Bread dough (page 146)

1 cup raisins

¾ cup walnuts, chopped

⅓ cup sugar, plus more for sprinkling over the top

Egg wash (1 egg beaten with 1 tablespoon of water), for brushing the loaf

1. **On baking day,** grease an 8½ × 4½-inch nonstick loaf pan.

2. **Sprinkle half the sugar over a silicone mat and set aside.** Dust the surface of the refrigerated dough with rice flour and pull off a 1½-pound (small cantaloupe–size) piece. Place the dough on the sugar-coated silicone mat. Sprinkle the remaining sugar over the top of the dough. Cover with plastic wrap and roll the dough out with a rolling pin until it is a ½-inch-thick rectangle.

3. Sprinkle the raisins and walnuts over the dough and roll it up, jelly-roll style, to incorporate them. Fold the ends into the middle to shape the dough into a ball.

4. Place the loaf in the prepared pan and smooth the surface with wet fingers. Cover loosely with plastic and allow to rest for 90 minutes (see sidebar in Master Recipe, page 70).

5. **Preheat the oven to 400°F.** (A baking stone is not required for loaf-pan breads, and omitting it shortens the preheat.)

6. Using a pastry brush, paint the top with the egg wash and sprinkle with sugar.

7. Place the loaf on a rack near the middle of the oven. Bake for **about 55 to 60 minutes,** or until golden brown. Smaller or larger loaves will require adjustments in baking time.

8. Remove from the pan and allow to cool on a rack before eating.

Vermont Cheddar Bread

Great cheese bread is a wonderful American specialty, and a complete meal in a slice (see color photo). The success of this loaf will depend on the cheese you use, so go with your favorite one.

Makes four 1-pound loaves. The recipe is easily doubled or halved.

Ingredient	Volume (U.S.), flour packed into measuring cups	Weight (U.S.)	Weight (Metric)
Mixture #1: Gluten-Free All-Purpose Flour (see page 60)	6 cups	2 pounds	910 grams
Granulated yeast	1 tablespoon	0.35 ounce	10 grams
Kosher salt[1]	1 to 1½ tablespoons	0.6 to 0.9 ounce	17 to 25 grams
Sugar (optional)	2 tablespoons	1 ounce	30 grams
Lukewarm water (100°F or below)	3½ cups	1 pound, 12 ounces	795 grams
Grated cheddar cheese, plus a slice for the top of loaf	1 cup	4 ounces	115 grams

[1]Can decrease (see page 25)

1. **Mixing and storing the dough:** Whisk together the flour, yeast, salt, and sugar (if using) in a 5- to 6-quart bowl, or a lidded (not airtight) food container.

Visit GFBreadIn5.com, where you'll find recipes, photos, videos, and instructional material.

2. Add the water and the grated cheese and gradually mix them in, preferably using a heavy-duty stand mixer fitted with the paddle attachment (see page 42). Mix for 1 minute, until the dough is smooth.

3. Cover (not airtight), and allow to rest at room temperature until the dough rises, approximately 2 hours.

4. The dough can be used immediately after the initial rise, though it is easier to handle when cold. Refrigerate it in a lidded (not airtight) container and use over the next 7 days. Or freeze for up to 3 weeks in 1-pound portions and thaw in the refrigerator overnight before use.

5. **On baking day:** Pull off a 1-pound (grapefruit-size) piece of dough. Place it on a pizza peel prepared with cornmeal (use plenty) or parchment paper. Quickly shape it into a ball and smooth the surface by gently pressing and smoothing with wet fingers. Cover loosely with plastic wrap or an overturned bowl and allow to rest for 60 minutes (see sidebar in Master Recipe, page 70).

6. **Preheat a baking stone near the middle of the oven to 450°F (20 to 30 minutes),** with an empty metal broiler tray on any shelf that won't interfere with rising bread.

7. Slash the top of the loaf, about ½ inch deep, with a wet serrated bread knife (see photos, page 70). Place a slice of cheese over the top of the dough.

8. Slide the loaf onto the hot stone. Pour 1 cup of hot tap water into the broiler tray, and quickly close the oven door (see page 31 for steam alternatives). Bake for **about 45 minutes,** or until richly browned and firm. Smaller or larger loaves will require adjustments in resting and baking time.

9. Allow to cool on a rack before eating.

VARIATION: CRISP CHEESY BREAD STICKS

To make thin crispy bread sticks (see color photo), follow the directions below with Vermont Cheddar Bread dough or any dough other than those in Chapter 9.

1. **Preheat the oven to 400°F.** Grease a baking sheet with oil or butter, or line with parchment paper. On a well-floured surface

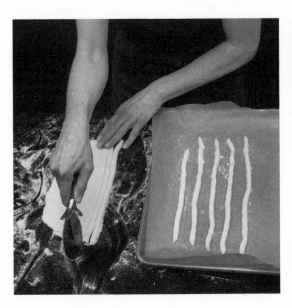

press out the dough into an 8 × 13-inch rectangle, about ⅛ inch thick, adding flour as needed to prevent sticking. Cut along the long side into ¼-inch-wide strips using a pizza cutter or sharp knife.

2. Very carefully pick up the strips (a long spatula is helpful) and lay them on the prepared baking sheet, spacing them about ½ inch apart. Drizzle olive oil over the strips and sprinkle with coarse salt, cheese, and/or herbs.

3. Bake the bread sticks in the middle of the oven for 10 to 16 minutes. The bread sticks are done when nicely browned and beginning to crisp; they will firm up when cool.

Wisconsin Beer-Cheese Bread

Beer bread is an old German specialty, and Wisconsin is famous for preserving two of the great traditions of its German immigrant ancestors—brewing and cheese-making. Beer is barley-based, and barley has gluten, so we didn't think we'd be able to adapt this one. Enter the gluten-free brewing industry. The gluten-free beers available today are not bad at all. Find one you like and use it here—you'll love the way it jump-starts yeasty flavors in the bread. The flavor of the bread gets even better when the dough has had a couple of days to brew.

Makes four 1-pound loaves. The recipe is easily doubled or halved.

Ingredient	Volume (U.S.), flour packed into measuring cups	Weight (U.S.)	Weight (Metric)
Mixture #1: Gluten-Free All-Purpose Flour (see page 60)	6 cups	2 pounds	910 grams
Granulated yeast	1 tablespoon	0.35 ounce	10 grams
Kosher salt[1]	1 to 1½ tablespoons	0.6 to 0.9 ounce	17 to 25 grams
Sugar (optional)	2 tablespoons	1 ounce	30 grams
Gluten-free beer, at room temperature	3 cups (two 12-ounce beers)	1 pound 8 ounces	680 grams
Lukewarm water	½ cup	4 ounces	115 grams
Grated sharp cheddar cheese	1 cup	4 ounces	115 grams

[1]Can decrease (see page 25)

Visit GFBreadIn5.com, where you'll find recipes, photos, videos, and instructional material.

1. **Mixing and storing the dough:** Whisk together the flour, yeast, salt, and sugar (if using) in a 5- to 6-quart bowl, or a lidded (not airtight) food container.

2. Add the liquid ingredients and the cheese, and mix with a spoon or a heavy-duty stand mixer fitted with the paddle attachment (see page 42).

3. Cover (not airtight), and allow to rest at room temperature until the dough rises, approximately 2 hours.

4. The dough can be used immediately after the initial rise, though it is easier to handle when cold. Refrigerate it in a lidded (not airtight) container and use over the next 7 days. Or freeze for up to 3 weeks in 1-pound portions and thaw in the refrigerator overnight before use.

5. **On baking day:** Pull off a 1-pound (grapefruit-size) piece of dough. Place it on a pizza peel prepared with cornmeal (use plenty) or parchment paper. Quickly shape it into a ball and smooth the surface by gently pressing and smoothing with wet fingers. Cover loosely with plastic wrap or an overturned bowl and allow to rest for 60 minutes (see sidebar in Master Recipe, page 70).

6. **Preheat a baking stone near the middle of the oven to 450°F (20 to 30 minutes),** with an empty metal broiler tray on any shelf that won't interfere with rising bread.

7. Dust the top with rice flour and slash, about $1/2$ inch deep, with a wet serrated bread knife (see photos, page 70).

8. Slide the loaf onto the hot stone. Pour 1 cup of hot tap water into the broiler tray, and quickly close the oven door (see page 31 for steam alternatives). Bake for **about 45 minutes,** or until richly browned and firm. Smaller or larger loaves will require adjustments in resting and baking time.

9. Allow to cool on a rack before eating.

Spinach Feta Bread

Spinach and feta cheese are usually seen wrapped in flaky phyllo pastry dough as savory Greek spinach pies. Our gluten-free bread version is hearty, satisfying, and much easier to make (see color photo).

Makes four 1-pound loaves. The recipe is easily doubled or halved.

Ingredient	Volume (U.S.), flours packed into measuring cups	Weight (U.S.)	Weight (Metric)
Mixture #1: Gluten-Free All-Purpose Flour (see page 60)	6 cups	2 pounds	910 grams
Granulated yeast	1 tablespoon	0.35 ounce	10 grams
Kosher salt[1]	1 to 1½ tablespoons	0.6 to 0.9 ounce	17 to 25 grams
Sugar (optional)	2 tablespoons	1 ounce	30 grams
Lukewarm water (100°F or below)	3¼ cups	1 pound, 10 ounces	740 grams
Cooked chopped spinach, squeezed dry	1 cup	6 ounces	170 grams
Crumbled feta cheese	¾ cup	4 ounces	115 grams
Cornmeal or parchment paper, for the pizza peel			
Water, for brushing the loaves			

[1]Can decrease (see page 25)

1. **Mixing and storing the dough:** Whisk together the flour, yeast, salt, and sugar (if using) in a 5- to 6-quart bowl, or a lidded (not airtight) food container.

2. Add the water, spinach, and cheese and mix with a spoon or a heavy-duty stand mixer fitted with the paddle attachment (see page 42).

3. Cover (not airtight), and allow to rest at room temperature until the dough rises, approximately 2 hours.

4. The dough can be used immediately after the initial rise, though it is easier to handle when cold. Refrigerate it in a lidded (not airtight) container and use over the next 5 days. Or freeze for up to 3 weeks in 1-pound portions and thaw in the refrigerator overnight before use.

5. **On baking day:** Pull off a 1-pound (grapefruit-size) piece of dough. Place it on a pizza peel prepared with cornmeal (use plenty) or parchment paper. Quickly shape it into a ball and smooth the surface by gently pressing and smoothing with wet fingers. Cover loosely with plastic wrap or an overturned bowl and allow to rest for 60 minutes (see sidebar in Master Recipe, page 70).

6. **Preheat a baking stone near the middle of the oven to 450°F (20 to 30 minutes),** with an empty metal broiler tray on any shelf that won't interfere with rising bread.

7. Dust with flour and then slash, about ½ inch deep, with a serrated bread knife (see photos, page 70).

8. Slide the loaf onto the hot stone. Pour 1 cup of hot tap water into the broiler tray, and quickly close the oven door (see page 31 for steam alternatives). Bake for **about 45 minutes,** or until richly browned and firm. Smaller or larger loaves will require adjustments in resting and baking time.

9. Allow to cool on a rack before eating.

Roasted Garlic Rosemary Bread

The Mediterranean is full of gluten-free delicacies: olives, olive oil, cheeses, chickpeas, legumes, and fabulous aromatic herbs like rosemary. Here's the bread to go with them.

Makes four loaves, slightly less than 1 pound each. The recipe is easily doubled or halved.

Ingredient	Volume (U.S.), flour packed into measuring cups	Weight (U.S.)	Weight (Metric)
Mixture #1: Gluten-Free All-Purpose Flour (see page 60)	6 cups	2 pounds	910 grams
Granulated yeast	1 tablespoon	0.35 ounce	10 grams
Kosher salt[1]	1 to 1½ tablespoons	0.6 to 0.9 ounce	17 to 25 grams
Sugar (optional)	2 tablespoons	1 ounce	30 grams
Rosemary	1 tablespoon fresh (1½ teaspoons dried)	—	—
Lukewarm water (100°F or below)	3½ cups	1 pound, 12 ounces	795 grams
1 head roasted garlic, squeezed out of its skin (see sidebar on page 162)			
Water, for brushing the loaves			
Cornmeal or parchment paper, for the pizza peel			

[1]Can decrease (see page 25)

1. **Mixing and storing the dough:** Whisk together the flour, yeast, salt, sugar (if using), and rosemary in a 5- to 6-quart bowl, or a lidded (not airtight) food container.

∽

Roast a head of garlic by wrapping it, unpeeled, in aluminum foil and baking for 30 minutes at 400°F. Allow to cool and cut across the top of each clove. Squeeze out the soft roasted garlic.

2. Add the water and roasted garlic, and mix with a spoon or a heavy-duty stand mixer fitted with the paddle attachment (see page 42).

3. Cover (not airtight), and allow to rest at room temperature until the dough rises, approximately 2 hours.

4. The dough can be used immediately after the initial rise, though it is easier to handle when cold. Refrigerate it in a lidded (not airtight) container and use over the next 10 days. Or freeze for up to 4 weeks in 1-pound portions and thaw in the refrigerator overnight before use.

5. **On baking day:** Pull off a 1-pound (grapefruit-size) piece of dough. Place it on a pizza peel prepared with cornmeal (use plenty) or parchment paper. Quickly shape it into a ball and smooth the surface by gently pressing and smoothing with wet fingers. Cover loosely with plastic wrap or an overturned bowl and allow to rest for 60 minutes (see sidebar in Master Recipe, page 70).

6. **Preheat a baking stone near the middle of the oven to 450°F (20 to 30 minutes),** with an empty metal broiler tray on any shelf that won't interfere with rising bread.

7. Brush with water, and then slash, about ½ inch deep, with a wet serrated bread knife (see photos, page 70).

8. Slide the loaf onto the hot stone. Pour 1 cup of hot tap water into the broiler tray, and quickly close the oven door (see page 31 for steam alternatives). Bake for **about 45 minutes,** or until richly browned and firm. Smaller or larger loaves will require adjustments in resting and baking time.

9. Allow to cool on a rack before eating.

Bagels

Traditional wheat bagels get their texture and flavor from a brief trip into a pot of boiling water before baking. So, we dutifully tested gluten-free bagels with a boiling step, but found that the boil just didn't make a difference. Here's an easier way to get your bagels-and-lox fix on a Sunday morning, even if you've gone gluten-free (see color photo).

Makes 5 bagels

1 pound (grapefruit-size portion) lean dough (any dough other than those in
    Chapter 9)
Poppy or sesame seeds, for sprinkling
Water, for brushing the bagels

1. **Preheat a baking stone near the middle of the oven to 450°F (20 to 30 minutes),** with an empty metal broiler tray on any shelf that won't interfere with the bagels.

2. Dust the surface of the dough with flour and pull off a 1-pound (grapefruit-size) piece. Divide the dough into 5 equal pieces and gently pat each piece into a ball with flour-dusted fingers.

3. Punch your thumb through the center of each dough ball to form a hole. Gently ease open the hole with your fingers and stretch until the diameter is about triple the width of the bagel wall. If the bagel breaks while you are opening the hole, you can press it gently back together.

4. Lay the bagels on the prepared baking
    sheet, cover loosely with plastic wrap, and
    allow to rest at room temperature for 20
    minutes.

5. Brush the bagels with water, sprinkle with
    seeds, and place the baking stone in the
    oven. Pour 1 cup of hot tap water into the
    broiler tray, and quickly close the oven door
    (see page 31 for steam alternatives). Bake
    for **20 to 25 minutes**, until richly browned
    and firm.

6. Allow the bagels to cool on a rack, then
    split and serve with your favorite bagel
    fillings.

Soft Pretzels

Pretzels are closely related to bagels, also having their origin in Central Europe (see color photo). You can make fantastic pretzels using our basic Master Recipe or any other lean dough, twisting it into the pretzel shape, which is a traditional symbol of earth and sun. We love them with mustard.

Makes about 5 pretzels

1 pound (grapefruit-size portion) Master Recipe dough (page 60)
Baking soda wash: 1 teaspoon baking soda mixed with ¼ cup water
Coarse salt, for sprinkling
Parchment paper, for the baking sheet

1. **Preheat a baking stone near the middle of the oven to 450°F (20 to 30 minutes),** with an empty metal broiler tray on any shelf that won't interfere with the pretzels. Prepare a baking sheet with parchment paper.

2. Dust the surface of the refrigerated dough with flour and pull off a 1-pound (grapefruit-size) piece. Divide the dough into 5 equal pieces. Gently elongate them by patting, squeezing, and rolling back and forth with your hands on a flour-dusted surface to form a long rope about 12 inches long, approximately ½ inch in diameter at the center, and tapered on the ends.

3. Directly on the prepared baking sheet twist the rope into a pretzel shape by first forming a horseshoe with the ends facing away from

you. Fold the tapered ends down to the thick part of the rope, crossing them one over the other. The ends should extend about an inch beyond the point where they cross.

4. Keep the formed pretzels covered loosely with plastic wrap as you repeat the process to make the rest. Let the pretzels rest at room temperature for 20 minutes.

5. Using a pastry brush, glaze the pretzels with baking soda wash and sprinkle with coarse salt.

6. Slide the baking sheet directly onto the hot stone. Pour 1 cup of hot tap water into the broiler tray, and quickly close the oven door. Bake with steam for **about 20 to 25 minutes,** until deeply browned and firm. If you want crisp pretzels, bake **5 to 10 minutes longer.**

7. Serve these a bit warm with a grainy mustard and a hefty stein of beer.

Visit GFBreadIn5.com, where you'll find recipes, photos, videos, and instructional material.

Bialys

Ah, oniony bialys! For both of us, these are a favorite taste of a mostly by-gone New York (see color photo). They used to be available in most every bagel store, but outside New York today, not so much (and less and less each day). A bit of cream cheese and you're ready for a lazy Sunday with the paper and coffee.

Makes about 5 bialys

1 pound (grapefruit-size portion) Master Recipe dough (page 60) or other
     lean dough (any dough other than those in Chapter 9)
1 tablespoon vegetable oil
½ onion, finely chopped
¾ teaspoon poppy seeds
Salt and freshly ground black pepper
Parchment paper, for the baking sheet

1. **On baking day:** Dust the surface of the dough and pull off a 1-pound (grapefruit-size) piece. Divide the dough into 5 equal pieces. Dust each piece with rice flour and quickly shape it into a 3-inch disk and rest on a parchment paper–lined baking sheet for 30 minutes.

2. **Preheat a baking stone near the middle of the oven to 450°F (20 to 30 minutes),** with an empty metal broiler tray on any shelf that won't interfere with the rising bialys.

3. While the dough is resting and the oven is preheating, in a skillet over medium heat, sauté the onions in the oil until they are

translucent and slightly golden. Don't overbrown at this stage, or they will burn in the oven. Remove from the heat and add the poppy seeds and salt and pepper to taste.

4. Using flour-dusted fingers, press the center of each bialy to flatten it, working your way out until there is a ½-inch rim of dough that is not pressed flat, and the bialy is about 4 inches wide. Fill the center of each bialy with 1 tablespoon of the onion mixture and press it gently into the bialy dough.

5. Transfer the baking sheet to the oven, pour 1 cup of hot tap water into the broiler tray, and quickly close the oven door (see page 31 for steam alternatives). Bake for **about 20 to 25 minutes,** until golden brown.

6. Allow to cool on a rack before eating.

8

FLATBREADS AND PIZZAS

Flatbreads are a great way to start your gluten-free five-minute baking adventures. They're the fastest breads we make because they need little or no resting time. And everybody loves pizza! Speaking of which, what's the difference between pizza and flatbread?

We're still struggling with that one. Clearly, if you make a flatbread that's something like Pizza Margherita, with basil, tomato, and mozzarella, it's pizza, the classic Italian pie. But from there it gets murky. Does the cheese make it pizza? Well, not really; the Italians use cheese in a lot of flatbreads that don't get named pizza.

Doesn't matter. Just enjoy.

Pizza and Flatbread Dough

This makes a delicious, tender and crispy crust, which works in all of our pizza and flatbread recipes.

Makes enough dough for ten 6-ounce pizzas or flatbreads (about 10 inches across). The recipe is easily doubled or halved.

Ingredient	Volume (U.S.), flour packed into measuring cups	Weight (U.S.)	Weight (Metric)
Mixture #1: Gluten-Free All-Purpose Flour (see page 60)	5 cups	1 pound, 11 ounces	755 grams
Cornmeal	1½ cups	9 ounces	255 grams
Potato starch	1 cup	6 ounces	170 grams
Xanthan gum or ground psyllium husk[1]	2 teaspoons	—	—
Granulated yeast	1 tablespoon	0.35 ounce	10 grams
Kosher salt[2]	1 to 1½ tablespoons	0.6 ounce	17 grams
Sugar	¼ cup	1¾ ounces	50 grams
Lukewarm water (100°F or below)	3¾ cups	1 pound 14 ounces	850 grams
Olive oil	½ cup	3¾ ounces	110 grams
Egg whites	4	4 ounces	115 grams
Cornmeal or parchment paper, for the pizza peel			

[1]Double quantity if using psyllium
[2]Can decrease (see page 25)

1. **Mixing and storing the dough:** Whisk together the flour, cornmeal, starch, xanthan gum, yeast, salt, and sugar in a 5-quart bowl, or a lidded (not airtight) food container.

2. Combine the liquid ingredients and add the mixture to the dry ingredients, using a spoon or a heavy-duty stand mixer fitted with the paddle attachment (see page 42), until all of the dry ingredients are well incorporated.

3. Cover (not airtight), and allow to rest at room temperature until dough rises, approximately 2 hours.

4. Dough can be used immediately after initial rise, though it is easier to handle when cold. Refrigerate in a lidded (not airtight) container and use over the next 5 days. Or store the dough for up to 2 weeks in the freezer in 1/2-pound portions. When using frozen dough, thaw it in the refrigerator overnight before use.

Neapolitan-Style Pizza Margherita (Basil, Tomato, and Mozzarella)

You can make a fantastic thin-crusted Neapolitan- (Naples-) style pizza from gluten-free dough (see color photo). Because great toppings are as much a part of the experience as the crust. Keep it thin and bake at your oven's highest temperature (500°F or 550°F) to achieve Italian-style crispness. Pizza Margherita is the standard all over Italy, with its tricolor toppings of tomato, basil, and mozzarella, mirroring the Italian flag.

Makes one 10-inch pizza; serves 2

6 ounces (large peach-size portion) of Pizza and Flatbread Master Recipe (page 172), or any dough other than those in Chapter 9

⅓ cup canned Italian-style chopped tomatoes, strained and pressed to drain liquid (or substitute a thick prepared tomato sauce)

3 ounces mozzarella cheese, cut into ½-inch chunks

6 fresh basil leaves, thinly slivered or torn

Coarse salt, for sprinkling

Gluten-free flour or cornmeal, for the pizza peel

1. **Preheat a baking stone to your oven's highest temperature (550°F or 500°F),** placing the stone near the bottom of the oven to help crisp the bottom crust without burning the cheese. Most stones will be hot enough in 20 to 30 minutes. You won't be using steam, so omit the broiler tray.

What makes tomato sauce a "pizza" sauce? It has to be a little thicker than typical tomato sauce, or drained of water—this helps avoid a soggy crust. In our Pizza Margherita, we strain away some of the water from canned chopped tomatoes to create a sauce with a rough, rustic effect. If you prefer a smooth sauce, process the tomatoes in a food processor, then reduce them in a saucepan over medium-low heat until thickened. Or make a thick and quick, slightly sweet sauce by food-processing one 6-ounce can of tomato paste with one $14^1/_2$-ounce can of tomatoes. This makes enough sauce for several pizzas and doesn't require draining or reduction of liquid to produce a thick, pizza-ready sauce.

Resist the temptation to use a lot of sauce on gluten-free pizzas, even if the sauce is nice and thick. Gluten-free dough is pretty wet in the first place, and using lots of sauce will make it difficult to get a crisp crust.

2. Prepare and measure all the toppings in advance. The key to a pizza that slides right off the peel is to work quickly—**don't let the dough sit on the peel any longer than necessary.**

3. Dust the surface of the dough and pull off a 6-ounce (large peach-size) piece. Quickly pat it into a ball on a pizza peel prepared with rice flour or cornmeal. Flatten it into a disk by gently pressing with flour-dusted fingers until you reach a

Visit GFBreadIn5.com, where you'll find recipes, photos, videos, and instructional material.

thickness of ⅛ inch. Check to be sure that the dough isn't sticking and, if it is, lift with a dough scraper and dust with more flour. As you work, pat the sides to round them off.

4. Spread the tomato over the surface of the dough with a spoon (a pastry brush works beautifully with smooth sauces). Do not cover the dough thickly, or your pizza will not crisp. As you add toppings, test for sticking by gently shaking the peel. The pizza should move freely. If it doesn't, use the dough scraper and add some flour to free it.

5. Scatter the mozzarella and basil over the surface of the dough, and give it a light sprinkling of salt to taste. **No resting is needed prior to baking—this can go straight to the preheated oven. Don't delay, or it might stick to the pizza peel.**

6. If you have an exhaust fan, turn it on now, because some of the flour or cornmeal on the pizza peel will smoke at this

∾

No-fail pizza crust roll-out: If you're having trouble flattening the dough with your fingers, try rolling it out between a sheet of parchment paper and plastic wrap. Brush the parchment paper with a teaspoon of olive oil in a 10-inch circle, place the dough on it, drizzle the top with more oil and cover with a piece of plastic wrap. Press or roll out to form a 10-inch circle. Check occasionally to be sure the dough is not sticking to the plastic wrap. If it is, just gently peel back the wrap and drizzle a tiny bit more oil. Once the dough is the right size, remove the plastic, cover with your toppings, and slide the pizza in the oven along with the parchment paper. For the crispest crust, carefully slide the parchment out from under the pizza once it's set, about 5 minutes into the baking.

To freeze the rolled-out raw crust: Roll out as instructed above, but use a second sheet of parchment instead of the plastic wrap. Don't worry if the dough sticks to the parchment, because it will be easy to remove once the dough is frozen. To bake the frozen pizza crust, just remove the top layer of parchment, top, and bake as directed. It may take a few more minutes than usual to become crisp.

Oven temperature: If you're using parchment paper be sure to match the oven temperature with the rating for the product you're using.

temperature (see sidebar, page 178). Place the tip of the peel near the back of the stone, close to where you want the far edge of the pizza to land. Give the peel a few quick forward-and-

Don't get smoked out of house and home: This recipe calls for an exhaust fan because there may be some smoke with such a hot stone. Make sure the stone is scraped clean before preheating. If you don't have an exhaust fan and smoke is a problem, choose a lower oven temperature (475°F) and bake 15 to 20 percent longer.

back jiggles and pull it sharply out from under the pizza. **Check for doneness in 8 to 10 minutes;** at this time, turn the pizza around in the oven if one side is browning faster than the other. It may need 5 minutes or more in the oven, depending on your pizza's thickness and your oven's temperature.

7. Let cool slightly on a rack to allow the cheese to set before serving.

VARIATIONS (see color photo)
Get creative! The Neapolitan Pizza recipe will work with any of your favorite toppings, or a combination. Remember to go easy on the quantity of topping, or your crust may be soggy. Here are some suggestions to get you started.

Fresh Tomatoes: Skip the canned tomatoes and try this with in-season fresh tomatoes, drained of seeds and liquid and thinly sliced. You can also roast the sliced tomatoes in a 400°F oven to evaporate the water, concentrate the flavor, and develop scrumptious caramelization in the tomato skin.

Sausage or Pepperoni Pizza: Layer sliced cooked sausage or pepperoni on top of the cheese in a basic tomato and cheese pizza. Rendering the sausage of some if its fat beforehand can make for a crisper crust. No need for extra salt when using sausage or cured meats.

Caramelized Onion and Manchego Cheese Pizza: This is a sophisticated combination of flavors, both sweet and savory. Use ½ cup of caramelized onions (step 1, page 114) covered with ⅓ cup of grated Manchego cheese.

Rustic Wild Mushroom and Potato Pizza Provençal: Here's a typically French take on pizza, though perhaps they'd do this kind of thing on a rich pastry base. The topping is made from:

2 small unpeeled red new potatoes, thinly sliced

6 large wild mushrooms, such as chanterelles, shiitakes, porcini, portobellos, or oyster mushrooms, or white mushrooms if wild are not available, thinly sliced

2 tablespoons olive oil

1 teaspoon herbes de Provence

Salt and freshly ground black pepper

5 oil-packed sun-dried tomatoes, thinly sliced

2 ounces finely grated Parmigiano-Reggiano cheese

Rice flour or cornmeal, for the pizza peel

1. In a skillet over medium heat, sauté the potatoes and mushrooms in the olive oil until the potatoes are soft. Season with the herbes de Provence and salt and pepper to taste.

2. Prepare the pizza crust as for Neapolitan Pizza (page 174).

Visit GFBreadIn5.com, where you'll find recipes, photos, videos, and instructional material.

3. Distribute the potatoes, mushrooms, and sun-dried tomatoes over the surface of the dough. Do not cover the dough thickly; the quantity specified will leave some of the dough surface exposed. Finish by sprinkling the cheese over the surface of the dough.

4. Bake as for Neapolitan Pizza (page 174).

Boule, Couronne, and Baguette—Master Recipe, page 63

Baguette, page 75

Couronne, page 80

Pain d'Epi, page 82

Baking in a Dutch Oven, page 33

Rolls, clockwise from top: Brötchen, Baguette buns, Pull-apart rolls, pages 91–92

100% Whole-Grain Loaf, page 102

Deli-Style "Rye" (Without the Rye), page 109

Caraway Swirl "Rye," page 112

Broa, page 137, and Yeasted Thanksgiving Cornbread with Cranberries, page 140

Spicy Pork Buns, page 142

From top: Oatmeal Maple Bread, page 146, Raisin-Walnut Oatmeal Bread, page 149, and Sunflower Seed Breakfast Loaf, page 253

Vermont Cheddar Bread, page 151

Crisp Cheesy Bread Sticks, page 153

Spinach Feta Bread, page 158

Clockwise, from bottom: Bagels, page 164, Bialy, page 168, and English Muffins, page 268

Olive Fougasse

Provençal *fougasse* and Italian *focaccia* share a linguistic and culinary background (see color photo). It's said that both may have ancient Greek or Etruscan roots. Fougasse distinguishes itself with artful cutouts that resemble a leaf or ladder; this delivers a crustier flatbread, with lots more surface exposed to the oven heat. As with focaccia, we bake it on a baking sheet to prevent oil from leaking all over.

Makes 6 appetizer portions

1 pound (grapefruit-size portion) Pizza and Flatbread Dough, Master Recipe (page 171), Olive Oil dough (page 122), or any lean dough (any dough other than those in Chapter 9)

¼ cup halved black olives

Olive oil, for brushing the dough

Parchment paper, for the baking sheet

1. **Preheat the oven to 475°F,** with an empty metal broiler tray on any other shelf. Prepare a baking sheet with parchment paper. (The baking stone is not essential; if you omit it the preheat can be as short as 5 minutes.)

2. Dust the surface of the dough with rice flour and pull off a 1-pound (grapefruit-size) piece, pat it into a ball, place it on a baking sheet prepared with oil or parchment and flatten it into a ½-inch-thick oval. As you work, pat the sides to round them off. Press in the olives.

3. Cut angled slits into the circle of dough (see color photo). You may need to add more flour to be able to cut the slits and keep them spread open adequately during baking so they don't close up. Gently pull the holes to open them. Brush the fougasse with olive oil and allow to rest for 20 minutes.

4. Place the baking sheet near the middle of the oven. Pour 1 cup of hot tap water into the broiler tray, and quickly close the oven door (see page 31 for steam alternatives). **Check for doneness at about 20 minutes** and continue baking, as needed, until golden brown.

5. Allow to cool on a rack before breaking off pieces and serving.

Fougasse Stuffed with Roasted Red Pepper

This is a very festive folded flatbread with a roasted red pepper filling (see color photo). It shares some of the same techniques used in making the olive *fougasse*, but the dough is folded over the roasted red pepper and slit to reveal the colorful filling inside. The rich and smoky red pepper perfumes the whole loaf. It's a fantastic and impressive hors d'oeuvre, sliced or just broken into pieces.

Makes 6 appetizer portions

1 pound (grapefruit-size portion) Pizza and Flatbread Dough (page 171), Master Recipe (page 63), Olive Oil dough (page 122), or any dough other than those in Chapter 9

1 red bell pepper, for roasting, or substitute equivalent amount of jarred roasted red pepper, drained and patted dry

Coarse salt, for sprinkling

¼ teaspoon dried thyme

Olive oil, for brushing the dough

Oiled parchment paper or a silicone mat, for the baking sheet

1. **Roast the red pepper:** Halve the pepper, discard the seeds, and flatten it, making additional cuts as needed. Grill or broil under a broiler or on a gas or charcoal grill, keeping the skin side closest to the heat source. Remove when the skin is blackened, 8 to 10 minutes. Drop the roasted pepper into a bowl or pot and cover it with plastic wrap. As it steams over the next 10 minutes, the skin will loosen. Gently hand-peel the pepper and discard the blackened skin. Some dark bits will adhere to the pepper's flesh, which is not a problem. Cut the roasted pepper into pieces.

2. **Preheat the oven to 475°F,** with an empty metal broiler tray on any shelf. Prepare a baking sheet with oiled parchment paper. (The baking stone is not essential; if you omit it the preheat can be as short as 5 minutes.)

3. Dust the surface of the dough and pull off a 1-pound (grapefruit-size) piece, pat it into a ball, place it on a prepared baking sheet and flatten it into a ¼-inch-thick oval. As you work, add flour to prevent sticking and pat the sides to round them off.

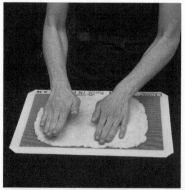

4. Place the roasted red pepper in a single layer on one side of the dough, leaving a ½-inch border at the edge. Fold the dough over to cover the pepper, and pinch to seal the edges. Using a knife, cut slits in the top crust to reveal the red pepper beneath. You may need to gently spread the holes open with flour-dusted fingers. Arrange the pepper so it peeks brightly through the windows.

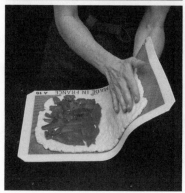
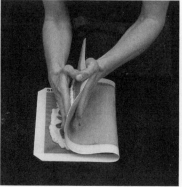
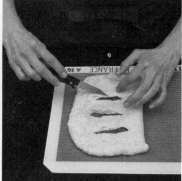

5. Brush the loaf with olive oil, and then sprinkle with salt and thyme to taste. Allow to rest for 20 minutes.

6. Place the baking sheet near the middle of the oven. Pour 1 cup of hot tap water into the broiler tray, and quickly close the oven door (see page 31 for steam alternatives). **Check for doneness at about 25 minutes** and continue baking, as needed, until golden brown, which may be 5 minutes longer. Fougasse will not develop a crackling crust because of the olive oil.

7. Allow to cool on a rack before, slicing and serving.

VARIATION: SPINACH AND CHEESE CALZONE

Traditional Italian-American pizzerias turn out these folded cheese pies using whole-milk ricotta, which makes for a richer and creamier filling, but part-skim versions also work well.

Makes 6 appetizer portions

$1/2$ pound (grapefruit-size portion) Pizza and Flatbread Dough (page 171), Master Recipe (page 63), Olive Oil dough (page 122), or any dough other than those in Chapter 9

1 large garlic clove, minced

1 to 2 tablespoons olive oil

$1/2$ cup fresh or thawed and drained frozen spinach leaves

1 large egg

1 cup whole-milk ricotta cheese

$1/4$ cup grated mozzarella cheese

$1/4$ teaspoon salt

Freshly ground black pepper

1. In a skillet over medium-low heat, briefly sauté the garlic in the olive oil until fragrant. Add the spinach and sauté for 2 minutes, until wilted. Drain and squeeze the spinach, discarding any liquid that may have accumulated.

2. In a bowl, beat the egg and then blend in the ricotta, mozzarella, salt, and pepper to taste. Mix the spinach with the cheese mixture.

3. Follow directions for Fougasse Stuffed with Roasted Red Peppers (page 183), omitting the red peppers and thyme, and fill with the cheese mixture instead. Don't slit the top crust—this is not a windowed flat-bread. Bake as directed.

Prosciutto and Olive Oil Flatbread

Pork fatback is one of life's great simple pleasures, and in Italy, it's used in hundreds of flavorful ways. One of the most interesting is in *pane di lardo*, in which the fatback studs a fabulous country bread. The lard from the pork melts into the bread and enriches a beautiful glistening crumb. Since your local supermarket isn't likely to carry Italian-style pork fatback, we've used a more universally available Italian meat in this gluten-free version of the original. Prosciutto is an aged Italian ham, but there are tasty domestic versions available as well. Spanish serrano ham is close to prosciutto in style, and can also be used. Rosemary complements the sweet and savory flavors of the meat for a fantastic flavor that goes beautifully with chilled Prosecco, an Italian sparkling wine—it's a sublime appetizer.

Makes 6 appetizer portions

1 pound (grapefruit-size portion) Pizza and Flatbread dough (page 172), Master
　　Recipe (page 64), Olive Oil dough (page 122), or any dough other than those
　　in Chapter 9

¼ teaspoon dried rosemary, crumbled, or ½ teaspoon fresh, chopped coarsely

2 ounces (⅛ pound/55 grams) sliced prosciutto or serrano ham, cut into 1-inch
　　squares

Olive oil, for brushing the top

Rice flour or cornmeal, for the pizza peel

1. Dust the surface of the dough and pull off a 1-pound (grapefruit-size) piece. Quickly pat it into a flattened ball on a work surface prepared with more flour. Press the rosemary and prosciutto into the surface and fold the dough over itself a few times until the rosemary is distributed.

2. Smooth the surface with wet fingers and flatten into a disk by gently pressing and patting until you reach a thickness of 1 inch. Check to be sure that the dough isn't sticking and, if it is, lift and dust with some flour. As you work, pat the sides to round them off.

3. Place the dough on a pizza peel prepared with rice flour or cornmeal. Cover loosely with plastic wrap or an overturned bowl and allow to rest for 60 minutes (see sidebar in Master Recipe step 5, page 70).

4. **Preheat a baking stone near the middle of the oven to 475°F (20 to 30 minutes),** with an empty metal broiler tray on any shelf that won't interfere with rising bread.

5. Brush with olive oil, and then slash the top, about ½ inch deep, using a serrated bread knife (see photos, page 70).

6. Slide the loaf directly onto the hot stone. Pour 1 cup of hot tap water into the broiler tray, and quickly close the oven door (see page 31 for steam alternatives). Bake for **about 30 minutes,** or until richly browned and firm. Smaller or larger loaves will require adjustments in resting and baking time.

7. Allow to cool on a rack before eating.

Focaccia with Onion and Rosemary

Onion, rosemary, and gluten-free olive oil dough: let's call it a new Tuscan tradition. Try this focaccia as a rustic antipasto or as an accompaniment to soups or pastas.

We bake focaccia on a rimmed baking sheet rather than directly on a stone, since oil would leak onto the stone and create an annoying problem with kitchen smoke. The key to success with this recipe is to go light on the onion. If you completely cover the dough surface with onions, the focaccia won't brown, and the result, though delicious, will be pale.

Makes 6 appetizer portions

1 pound (grapefruit-size portion) Pizza and Flatbread Dough (page 171), Master Recipe Dough (page 63), Olive Oil Dough (page 122), or any dough other than those in Chapter 9

Olive oil, for greasing a rimmed baking sheet

1/4 medium white or yellow onion, thinly sliced

2 tablespoons olive oil, preferably extra virgin, plus 1 teaspoon for drizzling

3/4 teaspoon chopped dried rosemary, or 1 1/2 teaspoons fresh

Coarse salt and freshly ground black pepper, for sprinkling the top

1. **Preheat the oven to 425°F,** with an empty metal broiler tray on any shelf that won't interfere with rising bread. Prepare a baking sheet with olive oil, parchment paper, or a silicone mat.

2. Dust the surface of the dough and pull off a 1-pound (grapefruit-size) piece. Quickly pat it into a ball on a work surface prepared

with rice flour. Smooth and flatten into a disk by gently pressing with your fingers, until you reach a thickness of ½ inch. Place on the prepared baking sheet.

3. In a skillet, sauté the onion slices over medium heat in 2 table-spoons of the olive oil until softened but not browned; if you brown them, they'll burn in the oven. Strew the onion over the surface of the dough, leaving a 1-inch border at the edge. Allow some of the dough surface to show through the onion; you may have some leftover onion at the end. If you can't see much dough surface, you're using too much onion and your focaccia won't brown attractively.

4. Sprinkle with the rosemary and coarse salt and freshly ground black pepper to taste. Finish with a light drizzle of the remaining 1 teaspoon olive oil.

5. After resting on the baking sheet for 20 minutes, place on a rack in the middle of the oven. Pour 1 cup of hot tap water into the broiler tray, and quickly close the oven door (see page 31 for steam alternatives). Bake for **about 30 minutes,** or until the crust is medium brown. Be careful not to burn the onions; cover them loosely with aluminum foil if they're browning too fast. The baking time will vary according to the focaccia's thickness. Focaccia will not develop a crackling crust, because of the olive oil.

6. Allow to cool on a rack, then cut into wedges and serve.

Sweet Provençal Flatbread with Anise Seeds

Provençal French bakers are famous for their savory flatbreads such as Pissaladière (page 225), but their lesser-known, gently sweetened breads are just as delicious. The anise, which has a distinctive licorice flavor, is a perfect complement to the orange zest.

Makes four 1-pound loaves. The recipe is easily doubled or halved.

Ingredient	Volume (U.S.), flour packed into measuring cups	Weight (U.S.)	Weight (Metric)
Mixture #1: Gluten-Free All-Purpose Flour (see page 60)	6 cups	2 pounds	910 grams
Granulated yeast	1 tablespoon	0.35 ounce	10 grams
Kosher salt[1]	1 to 1½ tablespoons	0.6 to 0.9 ounce	17 to 25 grams
Sugar	½ cup	3½ ounces	100 grams
Anise seeds	1 tablespoon, plus additional for sprinkling on the top		
Lukewarm water (100°F or below)	2¾ cups	1 pound, 6 ounces	625 grams
Orange juice	½ cup	4 ounces	115 grams
Olive oil, preferably extra virgin	¼ cup	2 ounces	55 grams
Zest of 1 orange			
Water, for brushing the loaves			
Oil, butter, or parchment paper, for the pizza peel			

[1]Can decrease (see page 25)

---

1. **Mixing and storing the dough:** Whisk together the flour, yeast, salt, sugar, and 1 tablespoon of the anise seeds in a 5- to 6-quart bowl, or a lidded (not airtight) food container.

2. Add the liquid ingredients and orange zest and mix with a spoon or a heavy-duty stand mixer fitted with the paddle attachment (see page 42).

3. Cover (not airtight), and allow to rest at room temperature until the dough rises, approximately 2 hours.

4. The dough can be used immediately after the initial rise, though it is easier to handle when cold. Refrigerate it in a lidded (not airtight) container and use over the next 10 days. Or freeze for up to 4 weeks in 1-pound portions and thaw in the refrigerator overnight before use.

5. **On baking day:** With wet fingers, pull off a 1-pound (grapefruit-size) piece. Quickly pat it into a ball on a baking sheet prepared with oil, butter, or parchment paper. Smooth and flatten into a disk by gently pressing with your fingers, until you reach a thickness of 1 inch. As you work, pat the sides to round them off.

6. Using a dough scraper (see page 37) or a pizza cutter, cut the round into several rough triangles for an authentic Provençal look. Space them about an inch apart, cover loosely with plastic wrap or an overturned bowl, and allow to rest for 40 minutes (see sidebar in Master Recipe step 5, page 70).

7. **Preheat a baking stone near the middle of the oven to 450°F (20 to 30 minutes),** with an empty metal broiler tray on any shelf that won't interfere with rising bread.

8. Brush the tops with water and place the baking sheet on the baking stone. Pour 1 cup of hot tap water into the broiler tray, and quickly close the oven door (see page 31 for steam alternatives). Bake for **about 35 minutes,** or until the crust is medium brown.

9. Allow to cool on a rack before serving.

Pine Nut–Studded Polenta Flatbread

Think of great Northern Italian food: polenta (coarse Italian-style corn-meal), olive oil, and pine nuts—no tomato sauce and mozzarella in sight. We wrapped those flavors up in a delightful bread that has crunch and gusto. You can make this with Broa dough (page 137), but the flavor will be more subtle and the texture less crunchy. This bread is fabulous passed as an hors d'oeuvre with olives or a nice Northern Italian firm cheese, like Asiago or *piave*.

Makes four 1-pound loaves. The recipe is easily doubled or halved.

Ingredient	Volume (U.S.), flour packed into measuring cups	Weight (U.S.)	Weight (Metric)
Mixture #1: Gluten-Free All-Purpose Flour (see page 60)	6 cups	2 pounds	910 grams
Coarse ground polenta meal	¾ cup	4½ ounces	130 grams
Pine nuts	½ cup	2.5 ounces	70 grams
Granulated yeast	1 tablespoon	0.35 ounce	10 grams
Kosher salt[1]	1 to 1½ tablespoons	0.6 to 0.9 ounce	17 to 25 grams
Sugar (optional)	2 tablespoons	1 ounce	30 grams
Anise seeds	1 tablespoon for dough, plus additional for sprinkling		

[1]Can decrease (see page 25)

(continued)

Ingredient	Volume (U.S.), flour packed into measuring cups	Weight (U.S.)	Weight (Metric)
Lukewarm water (100°F or below)	3¾ cups	1 pound, 14 ounces	850 grams
Olive oil, for brushing the top and greasing the pan			
Cornmeal or polenta, for the pizza peel			

1. **Mixing and storing the dough:** Whisk together the flour, polenta, pine nuts, yeast, salt, sugar (if using), and 1 tablespoon of anise seeds in a 5- to 6-quart bowl, or any lidded (not airtight) food container.

2. Add the water and mix with a spoon or a heavy-duty stand mixer fitted with the paddle attachment (see page 42).

3. Cover (not airtight), and allow to rest at room temperature until the dough rises, approximately 2 hours.

4. The dough can be used immediately after the initial rise, though it is easier to handle when cold. Refrigerate it in a lidded (not airtight) container and use over the next 10 days. Or freeze for up to 4 weeks in 1-pound portions and thaw in the refrigerator overnight before use.

5. **On baking day: Preheat the oven to 450°F,** with an empty metal broiler tray on any shelf that won't interfere with rising bread. Prepare a baking sheet with olive oil, parchment paper, or a silicone mat.

6. Using wet fingers, pull off a 1-pound (grapefruit-size) piece. Quickly pat it into a ball on the prepared baking sheet. Smooth and flatten it into a disk by gently pressing with your fingers, until you reach a thickness of 1 inch. As you work, pat the sides to round them off.

7. Rest on the baking sheet for 40 minutes, then brush with olive oil and sprinkle with additional anise seeds. Place on a rack in the middle of the oven. Pour 1 cup of hot tap water into the broiler tray, and quickly close the oven door (see page 31 for steam alternatives). Bake for **about 35 minutes,** or until the crust is medium brown.

8. Allow to cool on a rack, then cut into wedges and serve.

Za'atar Flatbread

Za'atar spice and *za'atar* bread are common in the Middle East, but they're still unfamiliar flavors in the United States (see color photo). Its lemony tang and distinctive flavor come from ground sumac berries, dried thyme, and sesame seeds. If you can't find it at a local Middle Eastern market, try Penzeys Spices by mail order or online (where it is spelled "zatar"). Or blend your own by mixing 1 part ground sumac berries, 2 parts dried thyme, and 1 part sesame seeds.

Makes 1 flatbread

1 pound (grapefruit-size portion) Pizza and Flatbread dough (page 172), Master Recipe dough (page 64), Olive Oil dough (page 122), or any dough other than those in Chapter 9

3 tablespoons olive oil, plus more for greasing the pan

1 tablespoon za'atar spice mix (see above)

Coarse salt, for sprinkling

1. Dust the surface of the dough, pull off a 1-pound (grapefruit-size) piece, and flatten the ball into a round, ½ to ¾ inch thick. Place the round on a baking sheet prepared with olive oil or parchment paper.

2. Sprinkle the za'atar spice mix over the dough round. Using your fingertips, poke holes into the surface of the dough at approximately 1-inch intervals. It's okay if the holes partially "refill" with dough as soon as your fingers are removed.

3. Drizzle the oil over the surface of the dough, taking care to fill indentations that remain from your finger-poking. Some of the

oil will run off the surface and find its way under the bread. Finish with a sprinkling of coarse salt, which accentuates the sourness of the za'atar. Use salt sparingly if your za'atar blend already contains salt.

4. **Preheat the oven to 475°F,** with an empty metal broiler tray on any shelf that won't interfere with the flatbread. Since you're not using a baking stone, the preheat may be as short as 5 minutes.

5. Rest on the baking sheet for 30 minutes and place the baking sheet on a rack in the middle of the oven. Pour 1 cup of hot tap water into the broiler tray, and quickly close the oven door (see page 31 for steam alternatives).

6. **Check for doneness at 15 minutes,** and continue baking until medium brown. Baking time will vary with the flatbread's thickness. Za'atar bread does not develop a crackling crust because of the oil.

7. Allow to cool on a rack, cut into wedges, and serve.

Pita

We were so excited when our gluten-free pita rounds puffed just as impressively as their wheat counterparts, because we'd been afraid that the puff had something to do with wheat's stretchiness (see color photo). Well, it doesn't. After a few failures, it turned out that the secret was a longer baking time. Ten extra minutes in the oven will dry it out enough to puff. People are sometimes surprised that the dough for pita isn't layered to encourage the puffing—it's not, you just use a thinly rolled dough disk. So why does it work? Since pita isn't slashed, internal steam is trapped inside. As soon as the top and bottom crusts set, steam in the interior pushes them apart. It can't miss. Pita is delicious warm from the oven—unlike loaf breads, it doesn't need to cool completely.

Makes one 9-inch pita, or two small individual pitas

¼ pound (peach-size portion) Pizza and Flatbread dough (page 172), Master Recipe Dough (page 64), or any dough other than those in Chapter 9 Rice flour, for the pizza peel

1. **Preheat a baking stone to 500°F (20 to 30 minutes).** You won't be using steam or a broiler tray and shelf placement of the stone is not crucial.

2. Sprinkle the surface of the dough with rice flour, pull off a ¼-pound (peach-size) piece, and place it on a pizza peel that has been generously sprinkled with rice flour. Pat it into a ball, then flatten it with your fingers. Continue until you have a ⅛-inch-thick round. Use a dough scraper to gently remove the round of dough from the peel if it sticks. Do not slash the pita or it will not puff. **No rise time is needed.**

3. Place the tip of the peel near the back of the stone, close to where you want the far edge of the pita to land. Give the peel a few quick forward-and-back jiggles and pull it sharply out from under the pizza.

4. Bake for **10 to 15 minutes,** or until lightly browned and puffed. You may need to transfer the pita to a higher shelf (without the stone) to achieve browning.

5. For the most authentic, soft-crusted pitas, wrap in clean dish towels and set on a rack to cool when baking is complete. The pitas will deflate slightly as they cool. The space between crusts will still be there, but may have to be nudged apart with a fork before you add favorite sandwich fillings.

6. Once the pitas are cool, store in plastic bags. Unlike hard-crusted breads, pita is not harmed by airtight storage.

Lavash Flatbread or Crackers

Armenian *lavash* is usually made as a big, wavy, very thin flatbread, baked until crisp and eaten with meals (see color photo). If you cut the dough into squares before baking, you'll have more of a flat American-style cracker. You can make these lean, or top them with oil, herbs, or seeds. A small amount of dough goes a long way because it's rolled so thin.

Makes two 12-inch sheets or at least 2 dozen 2-inch crackers

½ pound (orange-size portion) of any lean dough (any dough other than those in Chapter 9)

Olive oil, for drizzling

Sesame or other seeds, for sprinkling the top crust (optional)

Oiled parchment paper, for the pizza peel

1. **Preheat the oven to 400°F (20 to 30 minutes).**

2. Using wet hands, pull off a ½-pound (orange-size) piece of dough and place it on an oiled piece of parchment paper. Drizzle a small amount of oil over the dough and pat it into a disk. Drizzle the surface of the dough with more oil and cover it with plastic wrap. Using your fingertips or a rolling pin, press it into a ¹⁄₁₆-inch-thick rectangle.

3. Peel off the plastic wrap. **If you want to make crackers,** use a pizza cutter to score the dough into squares of the size you desire. Otherwise, proceed to the next step.

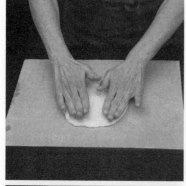

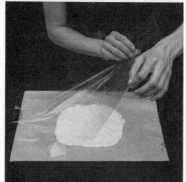

4. Transfer the parchment paper to a baking sheet. Sprinkle the dough with seeds, if using. Prick the surface all over with a fork to allow steam to escape and prevent puffing. **There's no need for resting time.**

5. Bake for **about 15 minutes,** or until golden brown. Since these are so thin, be careful not to scorch them when baking.

6. Allow to cool on a rack. Once cooled, they'll crisp, and they store well in airtight containers at room temperature.

Ksra (Moroccan Anise Flatbread)

This is a North African favorite from our first book, based on barley flour, which contains gluten. It's traditionally made from wheat flour, barley, and anise seeds, so converting this recipe was a challenge—the wheat **and** the barley had to go. (As much as we love them, anise seeds alone do not a bread make. We are not birds.) It turned out that flour milled from another typical African grain, millet, would fit the bill.

Makes four 1-pound loaves. The recipe is easily doubled or halved.

Ingredient	Volume (U.S.), flour packed into measuring cups	Weight (U.S.)	Weight (Metric)
Mixture #1: Gluten-Free All-Purpose Flour (see page 60)	6 cups	2 pounds	910 grams
Millet flour	1 cup	6 ounces	170 grams
Granulated yeast	1 tablespoon	0.35 ounce	10 grams
Kosher salt[1]	1 to 1½ tablespoons	0.6 to 0.9 ounce	17 to 25 grams
Sugar (optional)	2 tablespoons	1 ounce	30 grams
Anise seeds	1 tablespoon	¼ ounce	7 grams
Lukewarm water (100°F or below)	3¾ cups	1 pound, 14 ounces	850 grams
Water, for brushing the loaves			
Cornmeal or parchment paper, for the pizza peel			

[1]Can decrease (see page 25)

Visit GFBreadIn5.com, where you'll find recipes, photos, videos, and instructional material.

1. **Mixing and storing the dough:** Whisk together the flours, yeast, salt, sugar (if using), and anise seeds in a 5- to 6-quart bowl, or any lidded (not airtight) food container.

2. Add the water and mix with a spoon or a heavy-duty stand mixer fitted with the paddle attachment (see page 42).

3. Cover (not airtight), and allow to rest at room temperature until the dough rises, approximately 2 hours.

4. The dough can be used immediately after the initial rise, though it is easier to handle when cold. Refrigerate it in a lidded (not airtight) container and use over the next 10 days. Or freeze for up to 4 weeks in 1-pound portions and thaw in the refrigerator overnight before use.

5. **On baking day:** Dust the surface of the dough and cut off a 1-pound (grapefruit-size) piece. Place it on a pizza peel prepared with cornmeal (use plenty) or parchment paper. This dough does not stretch, so quickly shape it into a flattened ball about 1 inch thick, gently smoothing with flour-dusted fingers. Cover loosely with plastic wrap or an overturned bowl and allow to rest for 40 minutes (see sidebar in Master Recipe step 5, page 70).

6. **Preheat a baking stone near the middle of the oven to 475°F (20 to 30 minutes),** with an empty metal broiler tray on any shelf that won't interfere with rising bread.

7. Dust the top with rice or millet flour and slash, about ½ inch deep, with a serrated bread knife (see photos, page 70).

8. Slide the loaf onto the hot stone. Pour 1 cup of hot tap water into the broiler tray, and quickly close the oven door (see page 31 for steam alternatives). Bake for **about 30 minutes,** or until richly browned and firm. Smaller or larger loaves will require adjustments in resting and baking time.

9. Allow to cool on a rack before eating.

Naan

Ever think about why the Indian subcontinent is famous for its flat-breads? It's because the wheat traditionally grown there was low in gluten, so towering loaves of sandwich bread were not meant to be. But low in gluten is not low enough for gluten-free bakers, so we tested our gluten-free doughs using our tried-and-true naan method in a hot, cast-iron skillet, or a heavyweight nonstick skillet (see color photo). Butter or oil will work in lieu of Indian clarified butter (ghee), but the taste won't be as authentic. You can find ghee at South Asian or Middle Eastern markets.

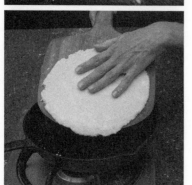

Makes 1 flatbread

¼ pound (peach-size portion) any lean dough such as Master Recipe (page 64), or any dough other than those in Chapter 9
1 tablespoon ghee, clarified butter, European-style butter, or oil
Ghee or unsalted butter, for brushing the loaf
Rice flour, for dusting the silicone mat and pizza peel

1. Dust the surface of the dough, pull off a ¼-pound (peach-size) piece of dough, and quickly pat it into a ball on a pizza peel prepared with rice flour. Smooth the surface and shape an 8-inch flattened disk by gently pressing with flour-dusted fingers. As you work, pat the sides to round them off.

2. Heat a heavy 8-inch cast-iron or other skillet over medium-high heat on the stovetop. When water droplets flicked into the pan skitter across the surface and evaporate quickly, the pan is ready. Add the ghee or oil.

3. Slide the disk into the skillet, decrease the heat to medium, and cover the skillet to trap the steam and heat.

4. **Check for doneness with a spatula at 3 to 5 minutes,** or sooner if you're smelling overly quick browning. Adjust the heat as needed. Flip the naan when the underside is richly browned.

5. Continue cooking, covered, for another 3 to 5 minutes, or until the naan feels firm, even at the edges, and the second side is browned. If you've rolled a thicker naan, or if you're using dough with whole grains, you'll need more pan time.

6. Remove the naan from the pan, brush with additional ghee or butter if desired, and serve with Indian foods or as an appetizer with prepared chutneys.

9

ENRICHED GLUTEN-FREE BREADS AND PASTRIES

This chapter shows what happens when a pastry chef and a doctor get together to develop scrumptious sweet and eggy baked treats that are gluten-free. Even if your diet has restrictions, you can still have homemade indulgences that make no apologies for skipping the wheat. And if you're trying to cut down on your sugars, you can experiment swapping sugar, honey, or agave with stevia, a sweet-tasting herbal extract (see page 29). **One technical word—we discovered that these enriched doughs were better when they were mixed in the stand mixer.** If you do use a spoon or dough whisk, mix vigorously. But if you're having trouble getting the light result you crave, break out the stand mixer.

Challah

Challah is the rich and delicious braided egg bread traditionally served in Jewish households at the start of the Sabbath, but nobody said you have to be Jewish to enjoy it (see color photo). It's really just one version of the many braided and non-braided, eggy festival breads that are common across cultures. With a little minor tweaking, our recipe can be the basis of gluten-free Finnish *pulla* or Norwegian *julekage* (see variations on pages 214–215).

The choice of melted butter versus oil definitely changes the flavor and aroma. For an intense and decadent challah, try making it with Brioche dough (page 216); the blast of butter and egg creates an incredibly rich effect (**but this will only work with brioche dough made from flour mixed with xanthan gum, not psyllium**).

Makes four 1-pound loaves. The recipe is easily doubled or halved.

Ingredient	Volume (U.S.), flour packed into measuring cups	Weight (U.S.)	Weight (Metric)
Mixture #1: Gluten-Free All-Purpose Flour (see page 60)	6 cups	2 pounds	910 grams
Granulated yeast	1 tablespoon	0.35 ounce	10 grams
Kosher salt[1]	1 to 1½ tablespoons	0.6 to 0.9 ounce	17 to 25 grams

[1]Can decrease (see page 25)

(continued)

Ingredient	Volume (U.S.), flour packed into measuring cups	Weight (U.S.)	Weight (Metric)
Lukewarm water (100°F or below)	2½ cups	1 pound, 4 ounces	565 grams
Honey or agave syrup	½ cup	6 ounces	170 grams
Large eggs	4	8 ounces	225 grams
Unsalted butter, melted, or oil	½ cup	4 ounces	115 grams
Egg wash (1 egg mixed with 1 tablespoon of water), for brushing the loaf			
Poppy or sesame seeds, for sprinkling			
Butter, oil, parchment paper, or a silicone mat, for the baking sheet			

1. **Mixing and storing the dough:** Whisk together the flour, yeast, and salt in a 5- to 6-quart bowl, or a lidded (not airtight) food container.

2. Add the water, honey, eggs, and melted butter (or oil), and mix with a spoon or a heavy-duty stand mixer fitted with the paddle attachment (see page 42).

3. Cover (not airtight), and allow to rest at room temperature until the dough rises, approximately 2 hours.

4. The dough can be used immediately after the initial rise, though it is easier to handle when cold. Refrigerate it in a lidded (not airtight) container and use over the next 5 days. Or freeze for up

to 3 weeks in 1-pound portions and thaw in the refrigerator overnight before use.

5. **On baking day:** Prepare a baking sheet with butter, oil, parchment paper, or a silicone mat. Dust the dough with rice flour and pull off a 1-pound (grapefruit-size) piece of dough. Cut into three equal-sized balls and gently roll and shape each ball into a 12- to 15-inch-long rope on a flour-dusted surface. Place the ropes on the prepared baking sheet.

6. Gently braid the strips, pinching the ends together.

7. Cover with plastic wrap or a roomy overturned bowl, and let rest for 45 minutes.

8. **Fifteen minutes before baking, preheat the oven to 350°F.**

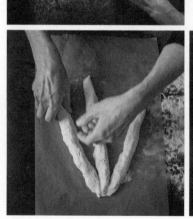

9. Brush the loaf with egg wash, and then sprinkle with poppy seeds. Bake until golden and firm, **35 to 40 minutes.**

10. Allow to cool on a rack before eating.

VARIATION: Turban-Shaped Challah with Raisins (see color photo)
Turban-Shaped Challah with Raisins is served during the Jewish New Year season, but similar enriched and fruited egg breads are part of holiday traditions all over the Western world, calling to mind the richer Italian Panettone (page 243), served at Christmas.

1. Press ¼ cup raisins into a 1½-pound piece of Challah dough (see page 210) by flattening the dough onto a piece of well-dusted parchment paper on a baking sheet. Gently form a single long, thin rope, tapering it at one end.

2. Starting with the thick end of the rope, begin forming a coil. When you have finished coiling, pinch the thin end under the loaf. Allow to rest and rise, as above, for 60 minutes (see sidebar, Master Recipe step 5, page 70).

3. **Fifteen minutes before baking preheat the oven to 350°F.**

4. Brush the loaf with egg wash (1 egg beaten with 1 tablespoon of water) and then sprinkle with sesame seeds. Bake for 35 to 40 minutes.

VARIATION: SCANDINAVIAN CHRISTMAS BREADS

Lightly enriched gluten-free dough like challah can be used as the basis for two terrific Scandinavian Christmas favorites: *pulla* (from Finland), and *julekage* (from Norway, Sweden, and Denmark). For a richer effect, try making them with Brioche dough (page 216). The secret's in the spices.

Finnish Pulla

Here's a great introduction to some of the cardinal spices of Scandinavian yeast baking. Add 1 teaspoon ground cardamom and ½ teaspoon ground anise seeds to the dry ingredients. Form, braid, and egg-wash the loaves as above, but sprinkle with **raw sugar** instead of poppy or sesame seeds and bake as above.

Norwegian Julekage

Add the same spices you used in pulla, plus ¾ cup dried fruits such as raisins, currants, cranberries, apricots, cherries, candied citron, candied lemon peel, or candied orange peel with the liquid ingredients.

Shape the loaf as a flattened round. After resting, bake at 350°F as above.

Meanwhile, make a simple icing by mixing together ½ teaspoon milk, ¼ cup confectioners' sugar, and ¼ teaspoon pure almond extract in a small bowl.

When the bread is baked and slightly cooled but is still warm, paint the loaf with the icing, and then sprinkle with toasted slivered or sliced almonds.

Brioche

The doomed Marie Antoinette is often quoted as having said, *"qu'ils mangent de la brioche,"* which means "let them eat brioche," not "let them eat cake—*gâteau!*" Historians have doubts about the true author of this quote, but in any case it was brioche on their minds and not cake.

Brioche can be enjoyed as a sweet bread with tea, as a breakfast pastry, or even as a flatbread base for savory toppings. Brioche is rich with butter, eggs, and a touch of honey. It is perfect no matter its shape—baked in a simple loaf pan or as a *brioche à tête* (see page 233)—and it is the inspiration for many of our pastry recipes.

Brioche dough made from flours that include psyllium (see page 61) becomes crumbly after refrigeration so they can only be baked in a loaf pan.

Makes enough dough for at least three 1¹/₂-pound loaves. The recipe is easily doubled or halved.

Ingredient	Volume (U.S.), flour packed into measuring cups	Weight (U.S.)	Weight (Metric)
Mixture #1: Gluten-Free All-Purpose Flour (see page 60)	2 cups	11 ounces	300 grams
Cornstarch	4¹/₂ cups	1 pound 6¹/₂ ounces	640 grams
Xanthan gum or ground psyllium husk[1]	2 teaspoons	—	—
Granulated yeast	1 tablespoon	0.35 ounce	10 grams

[1]Double quantity if using psyllium husk

(continued)

Ingredient	Volume (U.S.), flour packed into measuring cups	Weight (U.S.)	Weight (Metric)
Kosher salt[1]	1 to 1½ tablespoons	0.6 to 0.9 ounce	17 to 25 grams
Milk, warmed (100°F or below)	2¼ cups	1 pound, 2 ounces	510 grams
Large eggs, lightly beaten	4	8 ounces	225 grams
Honey	1 cup	12 ounces	340 grams
Unsalted butter, melted, plus butter for greasing the pan	1½ cup (3 sticks)	12 ounces	340 grams
Pure vanilla extract	1 tablespoon	½ ounces	15 grams
Egg wash (1 egg beaten with 1 tablespoon of water), for brushing the loaf			

[1]Can decrease (see page 25)

1. **Mixing and storing the dough:** Whisk together the flour, cornstarch, xanthan gum (or psyllium), yeast, and salt in the bowl of a stand mixer, or in any 5-quart bowl, or any lidded (not airtight) food container.

2. Add the milk, eggs, honey, melted butter, and vanilla, and mix with a spoon or a heavy-duty stand mixer fitted with the paddle attachment (see page 42).

3. Cover (not airtight), and allow to rest at room temperature until the dough rises, approximately 2 hours.

4. The dough can be used as soon as it's thoroughly chilled. Refrigerate it in a lidded (not airtight) container and use over the next 5 days. Or freeze for up to 3 weeks in 1-pound portions and thaw in the refrigerator overnight before use.

5. **On baking day:** Choose your pan. Brioche can be made in a 7-inch fluted brioche tin (page 40) or an 8½ x 4½-inch loaf pan (page 39); prepare the pan with butter. Using wet hands, pull off a 1½-pound (large grapefruit-size) piece of dough and drop it into the prepared pan. Smooth the top with water.

6. Cover with plastic wrap or a roomy overturned bowl, and let rest for 60 minutes (see sidebar, Master Recipe, step 5, page 70).

7. **Fifteen minutes before baking, preheat the oven to 350°F.**

8. Brush the top of the loaf with egg wash, and bake until golden and firm, **40 to 50 minutes.**

9. Allow to cool on a rack before eating.

Apple Cider Brioche

When we developed this dough we had apple cider doughnuts in mind (page 222). They were a favorite of Zoë's growing up in Vermont. If you can find fresh pressed cider, which is the apple juice you can't see through and which has a slightly tangy flavor, it will add a more intense apple flavor to your dough. Clear apple juice can be used in a pinch, but it's much sweeter and less flavorful. After we made doughnuts we tried the dough in a loaf pan and realized it was awesome, even without a fryer, so feel free to use this dough in any of our bread recipes in Chapter 9, especially the Apple, Pear, and Cranberries Coffee Cake (page 259).

Brioche dough made from flours that include psyllium (see page 61) becomes crumbly after refrigeration and can only be baked in a loaf pan.

Makes enough dough for at least three 1½-pound loaves. The recipe is easily doubled or halved.

Ingredient	Volume (U.S.), flour packed into measuring cups	Weight (U.S.)	Weight (Metric)
Mixture #1: Gluten-Free All-Purpose Flour (see page 60)	2 cups	11 ounces	300 grams
Cornstarch	4½ cups	1 pound, 6½ ounces	640 grams
Xanthan gum or ground psyllium husk[1]	2 teaspoons	—	—
Granulated yeast	1 tablespoon	0.35 ounce	10 grams

[1]Double quantity if using psyllium

(continued)

Ingredient	Volume (U.S.), flour packed into measuring cups	Weight (U.S.)	Weight (Metric)
Kosher salt[1]	1 to 1½ tablespoons	0.6 to 0.9 ounce	17 to 25 grams
Apple cider, warmed (100°F or below)	2¼ cups	1 pound, 2 ounces	510 grams
Large eggs, lightly beaten	3	6 ounces	170 grams
Honey	1 cup	12 ounces	340 grams
Unsalted butter, melted, plus butter for greasing the pan	1 cup (2 sticks)	8 ounces	225 grams
Pure vanilla extract	1 tablespoon	½ ounce	15 grams
Egg wash (1 egg beaten with 1 tablespoon of water), for brushing the dough			

[1]Can decrease (see page 25)

1. **Mixing and storing the dough:** Whisk together the flour, cornstarch, xanthan gum (or psyllium), yeast, and salt in the bowl of a stand mixer, or in any 5-quart bowl, or a lidded (not airtight) food container.

2. Add the apple cider, eggs, honey, melted butter, and vanilla, and mix them with the dry ingredients, preferably using a heavy-duty stand mixer fitted with the paddle attachment (see page 42).

3. Cover (not airtight), and allow to rest at room temperature until the dough rises, approximately 2 hours.

4. The dough can be used as soon as it's thoroughly chilled. Refriger-
    ate it in a lidded (not airtight) container and use over the next
    5 days. Or freeze for up to 3 weeks in 1-pound portions and thaw
    in the refrigerator overnight before use.

5. **On baking day:** Choose your pan. Brioche can be made in a
    7-inch fluted brioche tin (page 40) or an 8½ x 4½-inch loaf pan
    (page 39); prepare the pan with butter. Using wet hands, pull off a
    1½-pound (large grapefruit-size) piece of dough and drop it into the
    prepared pan. Smooth the top with water.

6. Cover with plastic wrap or a roomy overturned bowl, and let rest
    for 60 minutes (see sidebar, Master Recipe, step 5, page 70).

7. **Fifteen minutes before baking, preheat the oven to 350°F.**

8. Brush the top of the loaf with egg wash, and bake until golden and
    firm, **40 to 50 minutes.**

9. Allow to cool on a rack before eating.

Doughnuts

Doughnuts have become a national obsession (see color photo). There are local shops making all kinds of unique flavors with really high-quality ingredients. These are not the packaged variety of our youth. You can spend a pretty penny for a great doughnut and they're easy to make at home. You can follow these simple instructions and use any dough in Chapter 9 to create your own bakery-quality doughnuts. Some of our favorite doughs to fry are Apple Cider Brioche (page 219), Chocolate–Chocolate Chip Bread (page 256), Brioche (page 216), and Panettone (page 243).

Makes 5 or 6 doughnuts

1 pound (grapefruit-size portion) Apple Cider Brioche dough (page 219), Challah dough (page 210), or Brioche dough (page 216), defrosted overnight in the refrigerator if frozen

Vegetable oil, for deep-frying

Confectioners' sugar, for dusting

Special Equipment

Deep saucepan for deep-frying, or an electric deep fryer

Slotted spoon

Paper towels

Candy thermometer

1. Fill the saucepan (or electric deep fryer) with at least 3 inches

of oil. **Bring the oil to 360° to 370°F** as determined by a candy thermometer.

2. **As the oil is heating,** dust the surface of the dough with rice flour and pull off a 1-pound (grapefruit-size) piece. Dust the piece with more flour and flatten the dough into a ½-inch-thick rectangle on a floured surface. Using a doughnut cutter, cut the dough into 3-inch rounds.

3. Carefully drop the doughnuts in the hot oil, two or three at a time, so they have plenty of room to float to the surface. Do not over-crowd, or they will not rise nicely.

4. After 2 minutes, gently flip them over with a slotted spoon and deep-fry for another minute or until golden brown on both sides.

5. Using the slotted spoon, remove them from the oil and transfer to paper towels to drain.

6. Repeat with the remaining dough until all the doughnuts are fried.

7. Dust generously with confectioners' sugar.

John Barrymore Onion Pletzel

Pletzel or *pletzl* is a Yiddish word meaning "board" (Jeff's grandfather named this one after actor John Barrymore; no one knows why). It was a savory flatbread widely available in Jewish bakeries until about thirty years ago (see color photo). The pletzel flavors are a unique blend of onions and poppy seeds baked onto enriched and slightly sweetened dough. It is an Eastern European savory treat that is unforgettable when served with pot-roasted meats. Pletzel is perfect for mopping up that home-style gravy. Use the optional egg wash if you want to achieve a rich yellow color under the onions (see color photo).

Makes 1 pletzel

1 pound (grapefruit-size portion) Challah dough (page 210) or Brioche dough (page 216), defrosted overnight in the refrigerator if frozen

1½ tablespoons oil or unsalted butter, plus more for greasing the pan

1 small onion, thinly sliced

2 teaspoons poppy seeds

¼ teaspoon kosher salt

Egg wash (1 egg beaten with 1 tablespoon of water) (optional)

1. **On baking day:** Grease a baking sheet or line it with parchment paper or a silicone mat, and **preheat the oven to 400°F.** (A baking stone is not required, and omitting it shortens the preheat.)

2. With wet hands, pull off a 1-pound (grapefruit-size) piece of dough, and place it on the prepared baking sheet. Drizzle the

surface of the dough with oil and cover it with plastic wrap. Press it into a ½-inch-thick round.

3. Gently pull off the plastic wrap and allow to rest for 20 minutes.

4. Meanwhile, in a skillet, sauté the onion slices in the oil or butter until they just begin to color; don't overbrown, or they will burn in the oven.

5. If you're using the egg wash, paint it onto the surface of the dough with a pastry brush.

6. Strew the onions onto the pletzel and drizzle oil or butter over them (don't completely cover the surface with onions or the pletzel won't brown well). Finish by sprinkling the poppy seeds and salt over the onions.

7. After the pletzel has rested, place the baking sheet near the middle of the oven and bake for **about 35 minutes,** or until the pletzel has browned but the onions are not burned.

8. Allow to cool on a rack, then cut into pieces and serve.

VARIATION: *Pissaladière*

With a few deft changes, you can transform pletzel into a refined French onion tart.

1. Use only ½ pound of dough and press it out thinner, about ⅛ inch thick.

2. Finely chop the onion, and sauté it with a bay leaf, 4 chopped fresh flat-leaf parsley sprigs, ¼ teaspoon dried thyme (or ½ teaspoon fresh), and 2 large garlic cloves, chopped. Season with salt and pepper. Don't overbrown or the mixture will burn in the oven.

3. Remove the bay leaf and layer the dough with the onion mixture, then top with chopped anchovies to taste (we like at least 4 fillets), and 8 to 16 pitted and halved Niçoise or Kalamata olives.

4. Bake in a preheated **400°F** oven as on page 221—*voilà!* Check for doneness at 20 minutes.

Sticky Pecan Caramel Rolls

This is one of our most requested recipes, so converting this old wheat favorite to a gluten-free version was a priority. The rich, gooey caramel and nuts are rolled into our soft brioche dough and they form a sauce when inverted onto the serving platter. They are perfect for a special occasion, but easy enough for any day of the week (see color photo).

Makes 8 caramel rolls

The Dough

1½ pounds (small cantaloupe–size portion) Challah dough (page 210), Brioche dough (page 216), or Master Recipe dough (page 64), defrosted overnight in the refrigerator if frozen

The Caramel Topping and Filling

⅔ cup (1⅓ sticks) unsalted butter, melted, plus more for the pan

1 cup well-packed brown sugar

¼ cup honey

1 teaspoon ground cinnamon

¼ teaspoon freshly grated nutmeg

½ teaspoon salt

Pinch of freshly ground black pepper

2 cups whole pecans, toasted

1. **On baking day:** Mix together the melted butter, brown sugar, honey, cinnamon, nutmeg, salt, and pepper in a bowl. Grease a 9-inch cake pan with butter and spread half the caramel mixture evenly over the bottom. Scatter half of the whole pecans over the caramel mixture and set aside.

2. Dust the surface of the refrigerated dough with rice flour and pull off a 1½-pound (small cantaloupe–size) piece. Dust the piece with more flour and quickly shape it into a ball.

3. Press out the dough into a ¼-inch-thick rectangle. As you press out the dough, use enough flour to prevent it from sticking to the work surface.

4. Spread the remaining caramel mixture evenly over the rolled-out dough. Chop the remaining nuts into small pieces and sprinkle them over the top. Starting with the long side, roll the dough into a log and pinch the seam closed.

5. Using a very sharp serrated knife or kitchen shears, cut the log into 8 equal pieces and arrange over the caramel and pecans

Soft Pretzels, page 166

Neapolitan-Style Pizza Margherita, page 174 (top), and Variations, page 178

Fougasse Stuffed with Roasted Red Pepper, page 183, and Olive Fougasse, page 181

Za'atar Flatbread, page 197

Pita, page 199

Lavash, page 201

Naan, page 206

Braided Challah, page 210

Turban-Shaped Challah with Raisins, page 213

Doughnuts, page 222

John Barrymore Pletzel, page 224

Sticky Pecan Caramel Rolls, page 227

Cinnamon Buns with Cream Cheese Icing, page 230

Brioche à Tête, page 233

Almond Brioche (Bostock), page 236

Beignets, page 241

in the prepared pan, so that the swirled cut edge is facing upward. Allow to rest for 1 hour, loosely covered with plastic wrap.

6. **Fifteen minutes before baking, preheat the oven to 350°F.**

7. Place the pan on a baking sheet, in case the caramel bubbles over, and bake for **about 40 minutes,** or until golden brown and well set in the center. While still hot, run a knife around the edge of the pan to release the caramel rolls, and invert immediately onto a serving dish. If you let them set too long they will stick to the pan and will be difficult to turn out.

Cinnamon Buns with Cream Cheese Icing

These buns are filled with cinnamon-sugar, rolled up into spirals, and baked until the cinnamon and butter infuse the brioche dough. As if they aren't tasty enough on their own, we glaze the tops with rich cream cheese icing (see color photo).

Makes 8 buns

The Dough

1½ pounds (small cantaloupe–size portion) Challah dough (page 210), Brioche dough (page 216), or Apple Cider Brioche dough (page 219), defrosted overnight in the refrigerator if frozen

The Cinnamon Buns

¼ cup granulated sugar

¼ cup well-packed brown sugar

2 teaspoons ground cinnamon

1 teaspoon grated orange zest

3 tablespoons unsalted butter, melted

The Cream Cheese Icing

6 ounces cream cheese, at room temperature

⅓ cup confectioners' sugar

3 tablespoons heavy cream

1 teaspoon pure vanilla extract

½ teaspoon grated orange zest

1. **On baking day:** Dust the surface of the dough with rice flour and pull off a 1½-pound (small cantaloupe–size) piece. Dust the piece with more flour and quickly shape it into a ball.

2. Press out the dough into a ¼-inch-thick rectangle. As you press out the dough, use enough flour to prevent it from sticking to the work surface.

3. Mix together the granulated sugar, brown sugar, cinnamon, and orange zest in a small bowl. Brush the melted butter evenly over the rolled-out dough. Sprinkle the cinnamon-sugar mixture over the butter. Starting with the long side, roll the dough into a log and pinch the seam closed.

4. Using a very sharp serrated knife or kitchen shears, cut the log into 8 equal pieces and arrange on a baking sheet lined with parchment paper, so that the swirled cut edge is facing upward and they are at least 2 inches apart. Allow to rest for 1 hour, loosely covered with plastic wrap.

5. **Fifteen minutes before baking, preheat the oven to 350°F.**

6. Bake the buns for **about 30 minutes,** or until golden brown and set in the middle.

7. While the buns are baking, prepare the cream cheese icing by mixing all the ingredients in a bowl. Spread the icing over the buns after they come out of the oven.

8. Allow to cool on a rack before serving.

Brioche à Tête

Brioche à tête is a traditional French bread loaf, which is baked in a beautifully fluted pan and sports an extra little ball of dough at the top—the *tête*, or "head" (see color photo). Your guests will think you slaved over this one. The shape is ubiquitous in Parisian shops but quite rare elsewhere.

Makes 1 loaf or 8 small loaves

1 pound (grapefruit-size portion) Brioche dough (page 216), defrosted overnight in the refrigerator if frozen
Unsalted butter or oil, for greasing the pan
Egg wash (1 egg beaten with 1 tablespoon of water)

1. Grease a 7-inch fluted brioche pan or eight 2-inch brioche pans (see color photo).

2. Dust the surface of the refrigerated dough with rice flour and pull off a 1-pound (grapefruit-size) piece. Dust the piece with more flour and quickly shape it into a ball. (If you are making small loaves, divide the dough into 8 equal pieces and proceed as you would with a large loaf, with each of the small pieces of dough.)

3. Pinch off about one-eighth of the dough to form the tête (head) and set it aside. Place the larger ball into the prepared pan, and smooth out the surface with water; the pan should be about half full. Poke a fairly deep indentation in the top of this ball of dough. This is where you will attach the tête.

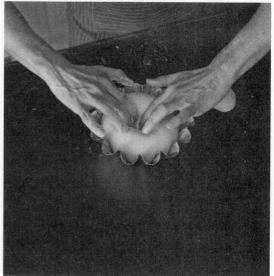

4. Quickly shape the small piece into a teardrop shape by rounding one end and tapering the other. Use plenty of rice flour to prevent the dough from sticking to your hands. Place the teardrop, pointed-side down, into the indentation of the dough in the pan and pinch the two together gently to ensure the tête stays attached during baking.

5. Allow to rest at room temperature for 60 minutes (30 minutes for the small loaves), loosely covered with plastic wrap.

6. **Fifteen minutes before baking, preheat the oven to 350°F.**

7. Brush the loaf with egg wash, and place it in the middle of the oven. Bake for **about 50 minutes (30 minutes for the**

smaller loaves), or until golden brown and well set. Smaller or larger loaves will require adjustments in resting and baking times.

8. Immediately remove from the mold and cool on a rack.

Almond Brioche (Bostock)

We adore *Bostock*, with its combination of buttery brioche, almond cream, and orange zest–infused sugar (see color photo). The traditional method involves baking brioche, slicing it, topping the slices with almond cream, and rebaking it. But that's just too much work for our five-minutes-a-day philosophy. We wanted the flavors without the extra work, so we rolled the filling into the dough and baked it just once.

Makes 1 loaf

The Dough

1½ pounds (small cantaloupe–size portion) Brioche dough (page 216), defrosted overnight in the refrigerator if frozen

Butter or oil, for greasing the pan

The Almond Cream

4 tablespoons (½ stick) unsalted butter, at room temperature

½ cup almond paste

¼ cup white rice flour

1 large egg

¼ teaspoon orange-flower water (optional)

¼ teaspoon almond extract

The Topping

¼ cup sugar, plus more for dusting the greased pan

Grated zest of ½ orange

½ cup sliced natural (raw and unsalted) almonds

1. **Make the almond cream:** Cream together the butter, almond paste, rice flour, egg, orange-flower water, and almond extract in a food processor until smooth and well combined. Set aside.

2. **Assemble the brioche:** Dust the surface of the dough with rice flour and cut off a 1½-pound (small cantaloupe–size) piece. Dust the piece with more flour and quickly shape it into a ball.

3. Press out the ball into a ¼-inch-thick rectangle. As you press out the dough, use enough additional flour to prevent it from sticking to the work surface.

4. Spread the almond cream evenly over the rectangle, leaving a 1-inch border all around. Roll up the dough, jelly-roll style, starting at the long end and making sure to seal the seam and the ends.

5. Generously grease an 8-inch round springform pan with butter. Sprinkle the greased pan with a dusting of granulated sugar.

6. Cut the dough log into 8 equal pieces with a very sharp serrated knife or kitchen shears. Place them evenly in the prepared cake pan so that the swirled cut edge is facing upward. Allow the dough to rest for 1 hour, loosely covered with plastic wrap.

7. **Fifteen minutes before baking, preheat the oven to 350°F.**

8. **Make the topping:** Mix together the sugar, orange zest, and almonds and sprinkle over the bostock. Place the springform pan on

a baking sheet, to catch any drips, and bake **about 45 minutes,** or until golden brown and well set in the center.

9. Run a knife around the pan to release the bostock while it is still hot and transfer it onto a serving dish. If you let it set too long it will stick to the pan.

Brioche Filled with Chocolate Ganache

This is the closest you'll ever get to bringing the aroma of a Paris pastry shop into your own kitchen. The rich brioche and smooth ganache reminds us of a *pain au chocolat*, without all the fuss and time. It makes a great treat for after meals or as a decadent breakfast with a cup of coffee.

Makes 1 loaf

1 pound (grapefruit-size portion) Brioche dough (page 216), defrosted overnight in the refrigerator if frozen

¼ pound bittersweet chocolate, finely chopped

2 tablespoons unsalted butter, plus more for greasing the pan

4 teaspoons unsweetened cocoa powder

1 tablespoon rum

⅓ cup corn syrup

Egg wash (1 egg beaten with 1 tablespoon water)

Granulated sugar, for sprinkling the top

1. **Make the ganache:** Melt the chocolate over a double boiler or in the microwave on low. Remove from the heat, add the butter, and stir until smooth. Add the cocoa powder, rum, and corn syrup to the chocolate mixture and whisk until smooth.

2. **Assemble the brioche:** Grease an 8½ × 4½-inch nonstick loaf pan. Dust the surface of the dough with rice flour and pull off a 1-pound (grapefruit-size) piece. Dust the piece with more flour and quickly shape it into a ball.

3. Flatten the ball into a ¼-inch-thick rectangle, dusting with flour as needed. Spread ⅓ cup of the ganache evenly over the rectangle, leaving a 1-inch border all around. Starting at the long end, roll up the dough and pinch the seam to seal.

4. Tuck the ends underneath the loaf and carefully lift the loaf into the prepared pan. Allow to rest for 60 minutes, loosely covered with plastic wrap.

5. **Fifteen minutes before baking, preheat the oven to 350°F.**

6. Brush the top with egg wash. Sprinkle lightly with granulated sugar.

7. Bake the brioche for **45 minutes,** or until the loaf is well set, the top is golden brown, and the sugar has caramelized. The bread may break open on top and reveal the ganache within.

8. Remove from the pan and cool completely on a rack; drizzle the remaining ganache over the top crust.

Beignets

Beignet is French for "fritter," or as we Americans like to call them, doughnuts. They're made from rich, yeasted dough, cut in squares, fried in oil, and then covered generously in confectioners' sugar. What's not to love? Here's a re-creation, using our simple recipe, of the sweet confection made famous by Café Du Monde in New Orleans (see color photo).

Makes 5 or 6 beignets

1 pound (grapefruit-size portion) Challah dough (page 210) or Brioche dough (page 216), defrosted overnight in the refrigerator if frozen

Vegetable oil, for deep-frying

Confectioners' sugar, for dusting

Special Equipment

Deep saucepan for deep-frying, or an electric deep fryer

Slotted spoon

Paper towels

Candy thermometer

1. Dust the surface of the dough with rice flour and pull off a 1-pound (grapefruit-size) piece. Dust the piece with more flour and quickly shape it into a ball.

2. Press the dough into a 1/2-inch-thick rectangle on a floured surface. Using a pizza cutter or knife, cut the dough into 2-inch squares.

3. Meanwhile, fill the saucepan (or electric deep fryer) with at least 3 inches of oil. Bring the oil to 360° to 370°F as measured with a candy thermometer.

4. Carefully drop the beignets in the hot oil, two or three at a time, so they have plenty of room to float to the surface. Do not over-crowd, or they will not rise nicely.

5. After 2 minutes, gently flip the beignets over with a slotted spoon and deep-fry for another minute or until golden brown on both sides.

6. Using the slotted spoon, remove the beignets from the oil and transfer to paper towels to drain.

7. Repeat with the remaining dough until all the beignets are fried.

8. Dust generously with confectioners' sugar and eat with a fresh cup of café au lait.

Panettone

Panettone is the classic Christmas bread sold all over Italy during the holidays (see color photo). It originated in Milan around the fifteenth century and has been the subject of much lore. The most commonly told story of how this bejeweled bread came to be goes something like this: A young nobleman falls in love with a baker's daughter named Toni. He disguises himself as a pastry chef's apprentice and creates the tall fruit-studded bread to present to Toni, calling it *Pan de Toni*. The bread is a success in the bakery and the father blesses the marriage.

The story is as rich and fanciful as the bread, made with dried fruit and the essence of lemons and vanilla. There are traditional panettone molds that are very high sided and come either straight or fluted. They can be found at cooking stores or on the web. You can use a brioche mold, but the bread won't have the classic high sides. Paper panettone molds are available from baking supply stores.

Panettone dough made from flours that include psyllium (see page 61) becomes crumbly after refrigeration.

Makes at least three loaves slightly larger than 1½ pounds each. The recipe is easily doubled or halved.

Ingredient	Volume (U.S.), flour packed into measuring cups	Weight (U.S.)	Weight (Metric)
Mixture #1: Gluten-Free All-Purpose Flour (see page 60)	2 cups	11 ounces	300 grams

(continued)

Visit GFBreadIn5.com, where you'll find recipes, photos, videos, and instructional material.

Ingredient	Volume (U.S.), flour packed into measuring cups	Weight (U.S.)	Weight (Metric)
Cornstarch	4 cups	1 pound, 4 ounces	565 grams
Xanthan gum or ground psyllium husk[1]	2 teaspoons	—	—
Granulated yeast	1 tablespoon	0.35 ounce	10 grams
Kosher salt[2]	1 to 1½ tablespoons	0.6 to 0.9 ounce	17 to 25 grams
Honey	1 cup	12 ounces	340 grams
Milk, warmed (100°F or below)	2¼ cups	1 pound, 2 ounces	510 grams
Large eggs, lightly beaten	4	8 ounces	225 grams
Unsalted butter, melted and slightly cooled	1 cup (2 sticks)	8 ounces	225 grams
Lemon extract	1 teaspoon	0.2 ounce	5 grams
Pure vanilla extract	2 teaspoons	0.4 ounce	10 grams
Lemon zest, grated	2 teaspoons	0.2 ounce	5 grams
Mixed dried and/or candied fruit[3]	2 cups	12 ounces	340 grams
Egg wash (1 egg beaten with 1 tablespoon water), for brushing the loaf			
Sugar, for sprinkling the top			

[1] Double quantity if using psyllium
[2] Can decrease (see page 25)
[3] Golden raisins, dried pineapple, dried apricots, dried cherries, and candied citrus, just to name a few that we've tried and loved in this bread.

1. **Mixing and storing the dough:** Whisk together the flour, corn-starch, xanthan gum (or psyllium), yeast, and salt in the bowl of a stand mixer or in a 5- to 6-quart bowl, or any lidded (not airtight) food container.

2. Add the honey, milk, eggs, melted butter, extracts, zest, and dried fruit, and gradually mix them into the dry ingredients, preferably using a heavy-duty stand mixer fitted with the paddle attachment (see page 42). The dough will be loose, but will firm up when chilled; **don't try to use it without chilling first.**

3. Cover (not airtight), and allow to rest at room temperature until the dough rises and collapses (or flattens on top), about 2 hours.

4. The dough can be used as soon as it's thoroughly chilled. Refrigerate it in a lidded (not airtight) container and use over the next 5 days. Or freeze for up to 3 weeks in 1-pound portions and thaw in the refrigerator overnight before use.

5. **On baking day:** Grease a 6-inch paper panettone mold or line a 6-inch round baking dish with greased parchment paper and grease the dish bottom, and tie the top of the parchment with kitchen string (see photo).

Visit GFBreadIn5.com, where you'll find recipes, photos, videos, and instructional material.

6. Dust the surface of the dough with rice flour and pull off a 1½-pound (small cantaloupe–size) piece. Dust the piece with more flour and quickly shape it into a ball. Place the ball into the prepared pan and smooth the top with water.

7. Allow to rest at room temperature for 60 minutes, loosely covered with plastic wrap.

8. **Fifteen minutes before baking, preheat the oven to 350°F.**

9. Remove the plastic wrap, brush the panettone with egg wash, and sprinkle with sugar. Bake for **50 minutes,** or until golden brown and hollow sounding when tapped.

10. Allow to cool on a rack before eating.

Buttermilk Bread

Many traditional American and British breads use buttermilk, which tenderizes the bread, creating a lovely soft crust and crumb, and a terrific flavor. It makes an ideal sandwich loaf, and it's heavenly in Cinnamon-Raisin Bread (page 249). You can also use this dough in any of the basic shapes we describe in Chapter 6, lowering the baking temperature to 375°F.

If you're using flour containing psyllium (see page 61), the dough will be crumbly after refrigeration, so it can only be baked in a loaf pan.

Makes two loaves, slightly less than 2 pounds each. The recipe is easily doubled or halved.

Ingredient	Volume (U.S.), flour packed into measuring cups	Weight (U.S.)	Weight (Metric)
Mixture #1: Gluten-Free All-Purpose Flour (see page 60)	2 cups	11 ounces	300 grams
Cornstarch	4 cups	1 pound, 4 ounces	565 grams
Xanthan gum or ground psyllium husk[1]	2 teaspoons	—	—
Granulated yeast	1 tablespoon	0.35 ounce	10 grams
Kosher salt[2]	1 to 1½ tablespoons	0.6 to 0.9 ounce	17 to 25 grams

[1] Double quantity if using psyllium
[2] Can decrease (see page 25)

(continued)

Ingredient	Volume (U.S.), flour packed into measuring cups	Weight (U.S.)	Weight (Metric)
Buttermilk, room temperature	2 cups	1 pound	455 grams
Large eggs, lightly beaten	4	8 ounces	225 grams
Honey	1 cup	12 ounces	340 grams
Oil, plus butter for greasing the pan	½ cup	4 ounces	115 grams
Pure vanilla extract	1 tablespoon	½ ounce	15 grams
Egg wash (1 egg beaten with 1 tablespoon of water), for brushing the top			

1. **Mixing and storing the dough:** Whisk together the flour, cornstarch, xanthan gum (or psyllium), yeast, and salt in a 5- to 6-quart bowl, or a lidded (not airtight) food container.

2. Add the liquid ingredients and eggs and mix with a spoon or a heavy-duty stand mixer fitted with the paddle attachment (see page 42).

3. Cover (not airtight), and allow to rest at room temperature until the dough rises, approximately 2 hours.

4. The dough can be used immediately after the initial rise, though it is easier to handle when cold. Refrigerate it in a lidded (not airtight) container and use over the next 7 days. Or freeze for up to 3 weeks in 1-pound portions and thaw in the refrigerator overnight before use.

5. **On baking day:** Grease an $8\frac{1}{2} \times 4\frac{1}{2}$-inch nonstick loaf pan. Using wet hands, pull off a 2-pound (cantaloupe-size) piece of dough, drop the dough into the prepared pan, and smooth the top with water.

6. Allow the dough to rest for 90 minutes, loosely covered with plastic wrap.

7. **Fifteen minutes before baking, preheat the oven to 350°F.**

8. Using a pastry brush, paint the top with egg wash. Bake the bread in the middle of the oven for **about 55 minutes,** or until golden brown.

9. Remove the loaf from the pan; if the loaf sticks, wait 10 minutes and it will steam itself out of the pan.

10. Allow to cool completely on a rack before slicing; otherwise, you won't get well-cut slices.

Cinnamon-Raisin Bread

Cinnamon-raisin bread is the ultimate comfort food. If you were once a child, you will love this bread (see color photo).

Makes one 2-pound loaf

1½ pounds (small cantaloupe–size portion) Buttermilk Bread dough (page 247), Challah dough (page 210), or Brioche dough (page 216)

Unsalted butter or oil, for greasing the pan

1½ teaspoons ground cinnamon

⅓ cup sugar

¾ cup raisins

½ cup chopped pecans or walnuts (optional)

Egg wash (1 egg beaten with 1 tablespoon water)

2 tablespoons sugar, for top of loaf

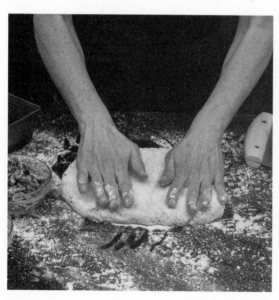 

1. Grease an 8½ × 4½-inch nonstick loaf pan. Dust the dough with rice flour and pull off a 1½-pound (small cantaloupe–size) piece of dough and quickly shape it into a ball.

2. Press out the dough into an 8 × 16-inch rectangle about ¼ inch thick, dusting with flour as needed. You may need to use a metal dough scraper to loosen the dough as you work.

3. Mix together the cinnamon and sugar and sprinkle the mixture evenly over the dough. Evenly distribute the raisins and nuts on top.

4. Starting from the short side, roll up the dough jelly-roll style. Pinch the edges and ends together, and tuck the ends under to form an oval loaf.

5. Place the loaf, seam-side down, in the prepared pan. Allow to rest for 90 minutes, loosely covered with plastic wrap.

6. **Fifteen minutes before baking, preheat the oven to 375°F.**

Visit GFBreadIn5.com, where you'll find recipes, photos, videos, and instructional material.

7. Brush the top lightly with egg wash and sprinkle with sugar. Bake for **45 to 50 minutes,** or until golden brown.

8. Remove the loaf from the pan; if the loaf sticks, wait 10 minutes and it will steam itself out of the pan.

9. Allow to cool completely on a rack before slicing; otherwise, you won't get well-cut slices.

Sunflower Seed Breakfast Loaf

This bread was inspired by a recipe from Thomas Gumpel, who was Zoë's bread instructor and friend from the Culinary Institute of America (see color photo). The first time she made the bread in his class, she'd been a bit impertinent and he decided to make an example of her. He had her mix the sunflower seed bread in an old-fashioned "bread bucket" (circa 1900) in the dining hall as public humiliation. The process took the better part of the class period, and Zoë's pride, albeit strong, took some abuse. But the bread was sublime. As harrowing as her first experience with this bread was, it's been a favorite ever since, but now it's gluten-free and only takes a fraction of the time to prepare.

If you're using flour containing ground psyllium husk (see page 61), the dough will be crumbly after refrigeration.

Makes two loaves, slightly smaller than 2 pounds each. The recipe is easily doubled or halved.

Ingredient	Volume (U.S.), flour packed into measuring cups	Weight (U.S.)	Weight (Metric)
Mixture #1: Gluten-Free All-Purpose Flour (see page 60)	2 cups	11 ounces	300 grams
Cornstarch	4 cups	1 pound, 4 ounces	565 grams
Xanthan gum or ground psyllium husk[1]	2 teaspoons	—	—

[1]Double quantity if using psyllium

(continued)

Visit GFBreadIn5.com, where you'll find recipes, photos, videos, and instructional material.

Ingredient	Volume (U.S.), flour packed into measuring cups	Weight (U.S.)	Weight (Metric)
Granulated yeast	1 tablespoon	0.35 ounce	10 grams
Kosher salt[1]	1 to 1½ tablespoons	0.6 to 0.9 ounce	17 to 25 grams
Sunflower seeds	1 cup, plus 2 tablespoons for top of the loaf	4¾ ounces	135 grams
Lukewarm milk (100°F or below)	2 cups	1 pound	450 grams
Honey	½ cup	6 ounces	170 grams
Sunflower oil (or vegetable oil), plus more for greasing the pan	⅓ cup	2.5 ounces	70 grams
Large eggs	4	8 ounces	225 grams
Egg wash (1 egg beaten with 1 tablespoon water) or water, for brushing the top			

[1]Can decrease (see page 25)

1. **Mixing and storing the dough:** Whisk together the flour, cornstarch, xanthan (or psyllium), yeast, salt, and 1 cup of the sunflower seeds in a 5- to 6-quart bowl, or a lidded (not airtight) food container.

2. Add the liquid ingredients and eggs and mix with a spoon or a heavy-duty stand mixer fitted with the paddle attachment (see page 42).

3. Cover (not airtight), and allow to rest at room temperature until the dough rises, approximately 2 hours.

4. The dough can be used immediately after the initial rise, though it is easier to handle when cold. Refrigerate it in a lidded (not airtight) container and use over the next 5 days. Or freeze for up to 3 weeks in 1-pound portions and thaw in the refrigerator overnight before use.

5. **On baking day:** Grease an $8\frac{1}{2} \times 4\frac{1}{2}$-inch nonstick loaf pan. Using wet hands, pull off a 2-pound (cantaloupe-size) piece and drop it into the prepared pan. Smooth the top of the loaf with more water. Allow to rest for 90 minutes, loosely covered with plastic wrap.

6. **Fifteen minutes before baking, preheat the oven to 375°F.**

7. Brush with egg wash, sprinkle the top with the remaining 2 tablespoons sunflower seeds, and slash, about $\frac{1}{2}$ inch deep, with a wet serrated bread knife (see photos, page 70).

8. Put the pan in the oven on a middle shelf and bake for **55 to 60 minutes,** or until richly browned and firm. Smaller or larger loaves will require adjustments in resting and baking time.

9. Remove the loaf from the pan; if the loaf sticks, wait 10 minutes and it will steam itself out of the pan.

10. Allow to cool completely on a rack before slicing; otherwise, you won't get well-cut slices.

Chocolate–Chocolate Chip Bread or Muffins

Chocolate bread is found in artisan bakeries all over the country (see color photo). Its origin is unknown, but we'd like to thank the chocophile who found yet another way to satisfy our chocolate cravings. The texture says bread, but chocolate cake lovers won't be disappointed.

If you're using flour containing ground psyllium husk (see page 61), the dough will be crumbly after refrigeration.

Makes at least three 1½-pound loaves or thirty-six 2-ounce muffins. The recipe is easily doubled or halved.

Ingredient	Volume (U.S.), flour packed into measuring cups	Weight (U.S.)	Weight (Metric)
Mixture #1: Gluten-Free All-Purpose Flour (see page 60)	2 cups	11 ounces	300 grams
Cornstarch	3¼ cups	1 pound	455 grams
Cocoa powder, unsweetened	¾ cup	4 ounces	115 grams
Xanthan gum or ground psyllium husk[1]	2 teaspoons	—	—
Granulated yeast	1 tablespoon	0.35 ounce	10 grams

[1]Double quantity if using psyllium

(continued)

Ingredient	Volume (U.S.), flour packed into measuring cups	Weight (U.S.)	Weight (Metric)
Kosher salt[2]	1 to 1½ tablespoons	0.6 ounce	17 grams
Milk, warmed (100°F or below)	2½ cups	1 pound, 4 ounces	565 grams
Large eggs, lightly beaten	4	8 ounces	225 grams
Honey	1¼ cups	15 ounces	425 grams
Unsalted butter, melted, plus butter for greasing the pan	1 cup (2 sticks)	8 ounces	225 grams
Pure vanilla extract	1 tablespoon	½ ounce	15 grams
Bittersweet chocolate, finely chopped	1½ cups	8 ounces	225 grams
Egg wash (1 egg beaten with 1 tablespoon of water), for brushing the top			
Granulated sugar, for sprinkling			

[2]Can decrease (see page 25)

1. **Mixing and storing the dough:** Whisk together the flour, cornstarch, cocoa powder, xanthan gum (or psyllium), yeast, and salt in the bowl of a stand mixer or in any 5- to 6-quart bowl, or any lidded (not airtight) food container.

2. Gradually add the milk, eggs, honey, melted butter, vanilla, and chocolate, and mix them in, preferably using a heavy-duty stand mixer fitted with the paddle attachment (see page 42).

3. Cover (not airtight), and allow to rest at room temperature until the dough rises for about 2 hours.

4. The dough can be used as soon as it's thoroughly chilled, at least 3 hours. Refrigerate it in a lidded (not airtight) container and use over the next 5 days. Or freeze for up to 3 weeks in 1-pound portions and thaw in the refrigerator overnight before use.

5. **On baking day:** Grease an 8½ × 4½-inch nonstick loaf pan or a 12-cup muffin tin. Using wet hands, pull off a 1½-pound (small cantaloupe–size) piece of dough (divide into 12 for muffins) and drop the dough into the prepared pan. Smooth the top with water.

6. Allow the dough to rest for 60 minutes (40 minutes for the muffins), loosely covered with plastic wrap.

7. **Fifteen minutes before baking, preheat the oven to 350°F.**

8. Brush the top with egg wash, and then sprinkle with sugar. Bake the bread in the middle of the oven for **about 50 minutes (30 for the muffins),** or until it is firm when you press on the top of the loaf.

9. Remove the loaf from the pan; if the loaf sticks, wait 10 minutes and it will steam itself out of the pan.

10. Allow to cool completely on a rack before slicing; otherwise, you won't get well-cut slices.

Apple, Pear, and Cranberry Coffee Cake

We like to bake with a combination of apples: some sweet and some tart, some that keep their shape and others that will break down and get saucy. Adding the pear lends a perfumey quality to the cake. If you make this with the Apple Cider Brioche dough, the flavor will be even deeper (see color photo).

Makes 1 coffee cake

The Streusel Topping

1 cup gluten-free oats

¾ cup white rice flour

1 cup well-packed brown sugar

1 cup chopped nuts (optional)

8 tablespoons (1 stick) unsalted butter, melted

Pinch of ground cinnamon

The Cake

1 pound (grapefruit-size portion) Brioche dough (page 216) or Apple Cider
   Brioche dough (page 210)

Unsalted butter, for greasing the pan

2 small apples (1 tart and 1 sweet), cored and thinly sliced

1 pear, cored and thinly sliced

1 cup cranberries

3 tablespoons brown sugar

Grated zest of ½ orange

1. **Make the streusel topping:** Combine all streusel ingredients in a
   bowl and mix until the butter is incorporated. Do not overmix—
   you want a crumbly texture. Set aside.

2. **Assemble the cake:** Grease an 8-inch round springform pan with butter. Set aside.

3. Toss the apples, pear, cranberries, brown sugar, and zest together in a small bowl and set aside.

4. Dust the surface of the dough with rice flour and pull off a 1-pound (grapefruit-size) piece. Divide the dough into two equal pieces, dust with more flour, and quickly shape them into rough balls.

5. Press the first piece of dough into the prepared pan.

6. Top with half of the apple and pear mixture, then sprinkle half of the streusel topping over it. Repeat with the next layer of dough, apple and pear mixture, and streusel.

7. Allow the cake to rest for 60 minutes.

Panettone, page 243

Cinnamon-Raisin Bread, page 250

Chocolate–Chocolate Chip Bread, page 256

Apple, Pear, and Cranberry Cake, page 259

Braided Raspberry Almond Cream Pastry, page 265

Greek or Turkish-Style Spinach Pie with Feta and Pine Nuts, page 267

Monkey Bread, page 270

Cinnamon Twists and Turns, page 272

8. **Fifteen minutes before baking, preheat the oven to 350°F.**

9. Bake the cake in the middle of the oven for **55 minutes.**

10. Allow to sit for about 15 minutes, then remove it from the spring-form pan.

11. Allow to cool on a rack before serving.

Blueberry–Lemon Curd Ring

This wreath-shaped pastry showcases the bright flavors of fresh lemon and the sweetness of in-season blueberries (see color photo). The delicious lemon curd is perfect for slathering on a hot piece of toast as well as for the filling of this pastry recipe.

Makes 8 servings

The Lemon Curd (makes 1 cup)
6 large egg yolks

1 cup sugar

1 tablespoon grated lemon zest

½ cup freshly squeezed lemon juice

8 tablespoons (1 stick) unsalted butter, cut into ½-inch slices

The Ring
1 pound (grapefruit-size portion) Brioche dough (page 216) or Challah dough
   (page 210)

1 cup fresh blueberries

Egg wash (1 egg beaten with 1 tablespoon of water)

2 tablespoons sugar, for dusting the top

1. **Make the lemon curd:** In a double boiler, over a low flame, whisk together all of the ingredients except for the butter. Stir continuously with a rubber spatula until the lemon curd begins to thicken, about 10 minutes.

2. Add the butter and continue to stir until it is completely melted and the curd is quite thick; it will be the consistency of smooth pudding.

3. If there are any lumps, strain the curd through a fine-mesh sieve into a container. Cover with plastic wrap and place in the freezer until cool, then refrigerate.

4. **Make the ring:** Line a baking sheet with parchment paper or a silicone mat dusted with rice flour.

5. Dust the surface of the dough with flour and pull off a 1-pound (grapefruit-size) piece. Dust the piece with more flour and quickly shape it into a ball.

6. On the prepared baking sheet, roll out the ball to a ¼-inch-thick rectangle. As you roll out the dough, add flour as needed to prevent sticking.

7. Spread ½ cup of the lemon curd evenly over the dough. Sprinkle the berries over the lemon curd.

8. Starting with the long side of the dough, gently roll it up into a log. Pinch the seam closed. Gently press the log until it is about 2½ inches thick. Carefully join the two ends together to form a wreath shape, dusting with additional flour if it gets sticky. Pinch the ends together to seal.

9. Allow to rest for 45 minutes.

10. **Fifteen minutes before baking, preheat the oven to 375°F.**

11. Brush away any excess flour. Using a pastry brush, paint the wreath lightly with egg wash, then generously dust with sugar. Make evenly spaced cuts all the way around the wreath, about 1½ inches apart. The cuts should be about ¼ inch deep.

12. Bake the ring in the middle of the oven for **35 to 40 minutes,** or until golden brown and well set. The top of the ring may break apart to reveal the lemon curd and blueberries.

13. Allow to cool on a rack before cutting.

Braided Raspberry–Almond Cream Pastry

Although this is easy to put together, the end result is dramatic and impressive for a special brunch or potluck (see color photo). If fresh raspberries are unavailable, feel free to show off seasonal fruits like apples, pears, peaches, and cherries.

Makes 1 braid

1 pound (grapefruit-size portion) Brioche dough (page 216) or Challah dough (page 210)

½ cup almond cream (pages 236, 237)

½ cup raspberry jam

1 cup fresh raspberries

Egg wash (1 egg beaten with 1 tablespoon of water)

Granulated white sugar, for sprinkling the top

Pearl sugar, for additional sprinkling (optional)

Parchment paper, for the baking sheet

1. Line a baking sheet with parchment paper or a silicone mat, and dust liberally with rice flour.

2. Dust the surface of the dough with flour and pull off a 1-pound (grapefruit-size) piece. Dust the piece with more flour and quickly shape it into a rough ball.

3. Roll out the dough on the prepared baking sheet into a ¼-inch-thick rectangle. As you roll out the dough, add additional flour as needed to prevent sticking.

4. Cover the center third of the dough with the almond cream, jam, and berries.

5. Using a pizza cutter, cut about twelve ½-inch-wide strips down each side. Gently lift and fold the strips, left over right, crisscrossing over the filling (see photo at left). Lightly press the strips together as you move down the pastry, creating a braid. Allow the braid to rest for 40 minutes.

6. **Fifteen minutes before baking, preheat the oven to 350°F.**

7. Brush lightly with egg wash, and then generously sprinkle with granulated sugar. Finish with pearl sugar, if desired.

8. Place the baking sheet in the middle of the oven. Bake the braid for **35 to 45 minutes,** or until golden brown.

9. Allow to cool on a rack before cutting.

SAVORY VARIATION: Greek- Or Turkish-Style Spinach Pie with Feta and Pine Nuts (see color photo)

Omit the almond cream, jam, raspberries, and sugar. Instead . . .

1. In a skillet over medium heat, sauté **1 pound chopped fresh spinach** in **1 tablespoon olive oil** until it's wilted and has given up a good amount of liquid, which you must squeeze-drain to prevent a soggy bottom crust.

2. Prepare and roll out the dough as on pages 265–266, and distribute ½ **pound crumbled feta cheese** down the center of the dough rectangle. Layer the drained spinach over the cheese.

3. Sprinkle ⅓ **cup pine nuts** over the spinach, then complete the braid as on page 266. Finish by brushing with **egg wash,** but omit the sugar topping and sprinkle with **black sesame seeds** (white seeds are fine, but the black ones are traditional in Greece and Turkey).

4. Allow to rest and bake as on page 266.

This variation also works with non-enriched doughs, which can be baked at 450°F for 20 to 25 minutes, but brush with water rather than egg wash.

English Muffins

The nooks and crannies of an English muffin are perfect for holding lots of butter and jam (see color photo). These are quick and easy, so they make a perfect last-minute breakfast treat. They are made on the stove, so there is no waiting for an oven to preheat, and their small size means only a minimal rest.

Makes five 3-inch muffins

1 pound (grapefruit-size portion) Challah dough (page 210) or Brioche dough (page 216)

3 tablespoons unsalted butter, for frying

1. Dust the surface of the dough with rice flour and pull off a 1-pound (grapefruit-size) piece. Dust the piece with more flour

and quickly shape it into a rough ball. Divide the dough into 5 equal pieces and shape them into balls, using enough flour to prevent sticking. Flatten the balls into disks and allow to rise for 20 minutes on a well-floured surface.

2. Heat half the butter in a large skillet on medium heat. Place 3 of the English muffins in the pan, making sure they have room to rise slightly.

3. Cook for about 5 minutes. When the bottoms are golden-brown and the muffins have puffed, flip them over and cook until the muffins are set all the way through and are nicely colored on both sides, about 10 minutes more. Repeat with the remaining butter and shaped dough.

4. Let cool on a rack before fork-splitting and serving.

Monkey Bread

Despite the silly name, this bread will be loved by kids and adults alike (see color photo). Rich brioche dough, tossed in cinnamon-sugar, then baked in caramel—who doesn't love that?

Makes 8 servings

1½ pounds (small cantaloupe–size portion) Challah dough (page 210), Brioche
    dough (page 216), or Chocolate-Chocolate Chip dough (page 256)
1 cup granulated sugar
1 tablespoon ground cinnamon
8 tablespoons (1 stick) unsalted butter, plus more for the pan
½ cup well-packed brown sugar
¼ teaspoon salt

1. Butter a 9-inch Bundt pan.

2. Dust the surface of the dough with rice flour and pull off a 1½-pound (small cantaloupe–size) piece. Divide the dough into two pieces. Dust them with more flour and gently shape each into a log, about 1½ inches in diameter. Cut the logs into ½-inch-thick slices.

3. Combine the granulated sugar and cinnamon in a large bowl. Drop the

dough slices into the bowl and coat them with the cinnamon-sugar. Roll the pieces into balls and place them in the prepared pan. Cover loosely with plastic and allow to rest for 60 minutes.

4. **Fifteen minutes before baking, preheat the oven to 350°F.**

5. Just before baking, melt the butter, brown sugar, and salt together in a small saucepan, stirring until completely smooth. Pour over the dough balls.

6. Place the pan in the oven on a baking sheet, just in case the caramel bubbles over the top. Bake for **45 to 50 minutes,** or until the top is golden-brown and the bread is set in the middle.

7. Invert the bread onto a serving plate and allow to cool slightly before serving.

Cinnamon Twists and Turns

This is a great recipe for leftover scraps of rolled-out brioche dough. The end result may look a bit like modern art, but the flavor will be a real treat—wonderful with a cup of coffee (see color photo).

Makes about 10 twists

$^{1}/_{2}$ cup sugar

$1^{1}/_{2}$ tablespoons ground cinnamon

1 pound (grapefruit-size portion) Challah dough (page 210) or Brioche dough (page 216)

Egg wash (1 egg beaten with 1 tablespoon of water)

1. **Preheat the oven to 375°F.**

2. Mix the sugar and cinnamon together in a small bowl.

3. Line a baking sheet with parchment paper or a silicone mat, and dust it with one-third of the cinnamon-sugar.

4. Dust the surface of the dough with rice flour and pull off a 1-pound (grapefruit-size) piece. Dust the piece with more flour and quickly shape it into a rough ball.

5. Press out the dough on the prepared baking sheet into a $^{1}/_{4}$-inch-thick rectangle. As you roll out the dough, add more cinnamon-sugar as needed to prevent sticking.

6. Sprinkle the dough with the remaining cinnamon-sugar. Using a pizza cutter, cut the dough into ¾-inch strips (if using a silicone mat, cut lightly to avoid cutting the mat). Carefully twist the strips into spirals and space them evenly on the baking sheet. Let rest for 15 minutes.

7. Bake for **20 minutes,** or until golden brown. Allow to cool. The sugar will have caramelized on the pan, so carefully break the Twists and Turns apart.

SOURCES FOR BREAD-BAKING PRODUCTS

෭෨

Bob's Red Mill: BobsRedMill.com, 800.349.2173
Cooks of Crocus Hill (St. Paul, Edina, and Stillwater, Minnesota): CooksOfCrocusHill.com, 651.228.1333, 952.285.1903, or 651.351.1144
Emile Henry cookware: EmileHenryUSA.com, 888.346.8853
King Arthur Flour: KingArthurFlour.com/shop, 800.827.6836
Le Creuset cookware: LeCreuset.com, 877.418.5547
Lodge Cast Iron cookware: LodgeMfg.com, 423.837.7181
Penzeys Spices: Penzeys.com, 800.741.7787
Red Star Yeast: RedStarYeast.com, 800.445.5746
Tupperware: Tupperware.com, 800.366.3800

SOURCES CONSULTED

American College of Gastroenterology, "Treatment of Celiac Disease: Gluten-Free Diet," http://patients.gi.org/topics/celiac-disease/, accessed September 20, 2013.

Behrman, R.E., Kliegman, R.M., and Jenson, H.B. *Nelson Textbook of Pediatrics*, 16th Edition. Saunders: Philadelphia, 2000.

Carroccio, A., Mansueto, P., Iacono, G., et al. "Non-Celiac Wheat Sensitivity Diagnosed by Double-Blind Placebo-Controlled Challenge: Exploring a New Clinical Entity." *American Journal of Gastroenterology* 2012; 107: 1898–1906.

Chang, K. "Gluten-free, whether you need it or not." *The New York Times*, February 5, 2013, http://well.blogs.nytimes.com/2013/02/04/gluten-free-whether-you-need-it-or-not/, accessed September 20, 2013.

Fasano, A., et al. "Prevalence of celiac disease in at-risk and not-at-risk groups in the United States—A large multicenter study." *Archives of Internal Medicine* 2003; 163(3):286–292.

Harvard Health Publications/Harvard Medical School. "Getting out the gluten: the super six." http://www.health.harvard.edu/newsletters/Harvard_Health_Letter/2009/June/Getting-out-the-gluten, accessed January 1, 2014.

Kupfer, S.S. "Making Sense of Marsh." *Impact*, a Publication of the University of Chicago Celiac Center, Fall 2009, http://www.cureceliacdisease.org/wp-content/uploads/2011/09/0909CeliacCtr_News_v3final.pdf, accessed September 20, 2013.

Mayo Clinic's Dr. Joseph A. Murray on differentiating celiac disease from gluten sensitivity, http://www.youtube.com/watch?v=p1fKaPkUtdk, accessed September 20, 2013.

Petersdorf, R.G., Adams, R.D., Braunwald, E., et al. *Harrison's Principles of Internal Medicine*, 10th Edition. McGraw-Hill: New York, 1983.

Rubio-Tapia, A., Hill, I.D., Kelly, C.P., Calderwood, A.H., Murray, J.A. "American College of Gastroenterology, ACG Clinical Guidelines; diagnosis and management of celiac disease." *American Journal of Gastroenterology* 2013; 108:656–676.

Rubio-Tapia, A., Ludvigsson, J.F., Brantner, T.L., Murray, J.A., Everhart, J.E. "The prevalence of celiac disease in the United States," *American Journal of Gastroenterology.* 2012 Oct; 107(10):1538–44.

Sapone, A., Bai, J., Ciacci, C. et al. "Spectrum of gluten-related disorders: consensus on new nomenclature and classification." *BMC Medicine* 2012;10:13.

Troncone, R., Jabri, B. "Celiac disease and gluten-sensitivity." *Journal of Internal Medicine* 2011; 269:582–90.

United States Food and Drug Administration. "Gluten-free labeling of foods." https://www.federalregister.gov/articles/2013/08/05/2013-18813/food-labeling-gluten-free-labeling-of-foods, accessed September 20, 2013.

University of Chicago Celiac Disease Center. "Jump Start Your Gluten-Free Diet: Living with Celiac/Coeliac Disease and Gluten Intolerance." R&R Publishing, 2011, http://www.cureceliacdisease.org/living-with-celiac/resources/jump-start-your-gluten-free-diet-ebook, accessed September 20, 2013.

U.S. Department of Agriculture Fact Sheet. "Egg Products Preparation: Shell Eggs from Farm to Table." http://www.fsis.usda.gov/wps/portal/fsis /topics/food-safety-education/get-answers/food-safety-fact-sheets/egg -products-preparation/shell-eggs-from-farm-to-table, accessed September 20, 2013.

INDEX